The Internal History of English:
Linguistic Changes

The Internal History of English: Linguistic Changes

1판1쇄 발행 2019년 8월 31일

지 은 이   이 필 환
펴 낸 이   김 진 수
펴 낸 곳   **한국문화사**
등   록   제1994-9호
주   소   서울특별시 성동구 광나루로 130 서울숲 IT캐슬 1310호
전   화   02-464-7708
팩   스   02-499-0846
이 메 일   hkm7708@hanmail.net
홈페이지   www.hankookmunhwasa.co.kr

책값은 뒤표지에 있습니다.

잘못된 책은 구매처에서 바꾸어 드립니다.
이 책의 내용은 저작권법에 따라 보호받고 있습니다.

ISBN 978-89-6817-790-3 93740

이 도서의 국립중앙도서관 출판예정도서목록(CIP)은 서지정보유통지원시스템
홈페이지(http://seoji.nl.go.kr)와 국가자료공동목록시스템(http://www.nl.go.kr/kolisnet)에서
이용하실 수 있습니다.(CIP제어번호: CIP2019032043)

The Internal History of English:
Linguistic Changes

PIL-HWAN LEE

한국문화사

PIL-HWAN LEE is Professor in the Department of English Language and Literature at Keimyung University, where he has taught since 2000. Before that, he worked for Chonbuk Sanup University for more than six years (1994-2000). He has held visiting appointments at the University of Manchester (supported by the British Council Fellowship, 1998-1999) and the California State University (Fresno, 2005). He graduated from the Department of English Language and Literature at Seoul National University (1986), and did his PhD there, too (1993, *A Diachronic Study on Word Order in English: The Minimalist Approach*).

He is the author of *English Diachronic Syntax* (1999, Excellent Authorship by the Korean Ministry of Culture, Sports and Tourism) and *Syntactic Changes in English* (2007, Excellent Authorship by the Korean Ministry of Culture, Sports and Tourism). He was the chief-editor of the journal *English Language and Linguistics* and was the president of the English Linguistics Society of Korea (2015-2017). His research efforts have focussed on English historical syntax and English grammar. He has written more than forty articles on these subjects.

■ Preface

Why do we have to study **the history of English**?

There are already so many books on the history of English, both large and small, that this book seems redundant and unnecessary. What is more, this book does rarely give new academic findings on the topic. Nevertheless, I decided to make this book to be brought into the world, since it was written for pedagogical purposes, not for strictly academic ones. The main readers of this book will be Korean university students. These days, we, Korean professors, are forced to take such 'practical' classes like TOEIC, English Composition, English Grammar, etc., as the major courses of the Department of English and, at the same time, are pressed to give up teaching the so-called 'academic' subjects, including the history of English. "Most English-language courses, nowadays, are either concerned with developing a practical competence or with understanding the synchronic structure of English" (Rastall 2002: 31).

There is a prediction that artificial intelligence will overcome language barriers as a tool beyond what we can imagine in a near future. The barriers of language will soon disappear, and the day of liberation from the difficulty and boredom of learning foreign languages is not far. Then we may not have to waste time and effort in studying English. The purpose of language education is not to secure 'communication tools', however, but to provide an opportunity for the mutual understanding of the culture and the promotion of the individual's cultivation to alleviate the conflict and to eliminate its cause. From this point of view, the meaning of learning the history of English is revealed. It is an attempt to understand the whole English-American culture.

Nevertheless, the history of English was taught too atomistically without the proper connection with contemporary English. So I believe that what matters is not the course itself but the teaching method and textbooks for the course. For "English in Historical Perspective", advocated by Rastall (2002), the history of English should be taught at a university-level, at least for the students of English major. In spite of the need to seek for the explanation of contemporary English usage in a historical light, we did not achieve this goal at the courses of the Department of English. This situation is severely observed in the non-native environment, as at Korean universities. It is a greatly worrying situation that the students' interest in English linguistics (not the study of the so-called 'practical' English), English literature, or the humanities in general, has recently been weakening in Korea. However, I am confident that the study of the history of English will be of great help in studying contemporary 'practical' English, too.

This book was written to be used as a(n easy) textbook for the graduate course of the history of English at Korean Universities. This book deals with the 'internal' history of English in a more detailed way than most other introductory textbooks in this field; phonological, morphological, semantic and syntactic changes, since I hope that this book will be used as a starting material for the students of graduate level to find some interesting research topics here. For the 'external' history of English, it is recommended to refer to the separate volume, titled *The External History of English: Stories of English*.

Lastly, I should confess that I feel uneasy in publishing this book, because I am greatly worried about the possibility of infringing copyright. This book contains not a few direct quotations. I have tried to reveal all the primary sources of the quotations, but it was limited and not always possible. I apologize for any infringement of copyright, if any.

Pil-Hwan Lee

Youngam Hall, Keimyung University, January 2019

C·O·N·T·E·N·T·S

Preface __ 5

CHAPTER 1. Language Change __ 9
    1.1. Language-external Causes for Language Change ·············· 10
    1.2. Language-internal Causes for Language Change ·············· 15

CHAPTER 2. Changes in Vocabulary: Lexical Change __ 21
    2.1. Borrowing Words from Foreign Sources ························· 22
    2.2. Creating Words from Native Sources ···························· 39
    2.3. Current Changes in English Vocabulary ························· 46

CHAPTER 3. Changes in Spelling and Pronunciation:
                Orthographic and Phonetic Change __ 49
    3.1. Spelling Change ··· 56
    3.2. Pronunciation Change ·· 68
    3.3. Remedies for Discrepancy: Efforts for Spelling Reforms ····· 77

CHAPTER 4. Changes in Word Form: Morphological Change __ 81
    4.1. Inflection: Declension and Conjugation ··························· 81
    4.2. Pronouns ··· 86
    4.3. Articles and Demonstratives ··· 99
    4.4. Nouns ·· 101
    4.5. Adjectives and Adverbs ·· 106
    4.6. Verbs ··· 110

CHAPTER 5. Changes in Grammar: Syntactic Change __ 117

    5.1. Word Order ·· 118
    5.2. Internal Structure of the Noun Phrase ····················· 124
    5.3. Internal Structure of the Verb Phrase ······················ 131
    5.4. Grammatical Functions ······································ 153

CHAPTER 6. Changes in Meaning: Semantic Change __ 165

    6.1. Aspects of Meaning ·· 165
    6.2. Metaphoric and Metonymic Transfer of Meaning ············ 167
    6.3. Synesthesia ·· 169
    6.4. Abstraction of Meaning ···································· 170
    6.5. Objectivization and Subjectivization of Meaning ············ 171
    6.6. Broadening and Narrowing ································· 172
    6.7. Pejoration and Amelioration ································ 175
    6.8. Taboo and Euphemism ····································· 177
    6.9. Semantic Bleaching ·· 179
    6.10. Why does Meaning Change? ······························· 180
    6.11. Meaning Change and Dictionaries ························· 182

Cited Bibliography __ 184

Index __ 188

Chapter 01

Language Change

Every language changes in the flow of time. English is also changing all the time. New words, new pronunciations, and even new grammatical forms are constantly coming into use. At the same time, old words, old pronunciations, and old grammatical forms are gradually disappearing. It is the normal state of language. Language change cannot be halted. Languages are self-regulating systems which can be left to take care of themselves. In this sense, language is a living creature, to which change is a fate.[1]

Then, why does language change?[2] Language changes for a wide variety of reasons. Although we are greatly curious about why language changes, it is not answered satisfactorily as yet.[3] Nevertheless, various reasons and

---

1) "Change is natural because a language system is culturally transmitted. Like other conventional matters - such as fashions of clothing, cooking, entertainment, means of livelihood, and government - language is undergoing revision constantly." (Pyles and Algeo 1993: 13)

2) Since the explanation of language change is a topic of much debate and considerable disagreement, its full treatment is beyond the cover of this introductory book.

3) "Until the early 1970s, it was common to find statements in historical linguistic

causal factors have been guessed and proposed.[4] The various reasons for language change can be grouped into two; one is the language-internal causes, and the other is language-external ones. "Internal causes are determined for the most part by physical realities of human biology, by the limitations on control of the speech organs and on what humans are able to distinguish with their hearing or are able to process with their cognitive make-up," while "external causes of change involve factors that are largely outside the structure of language itself and outside the human organism" (Campbell 2001: 285-86). In the last centuries, when the scientific study of human languages was not much developed, such factors as climate, geography, race, anatomical features of human body, etiquette, social conventions, and even indolence were mentioned as possible causal factors for language change.[5] However, the factors influence each other, since there is a close relation between a language and the society where it is spoken. To fully understand language change, a broad view of language is required which considers these two aspects together.

1.1. Language-external Causes for Language Change

Let us consider language-external causes first. First of all, the contact with a foreign language can cause language change. When two languages are

---

works to the effect that we should be concerned with 'how' languages change, but that the question of 'why' languages change could not be answered and therefore should be avoided." (Campbell 2001: 282)

4) *Causal factors* mean "factors which always bring about change and those which create circumstances which are known to facilitate change." (Campbell 2001: 283)

5) The examples for each case are given in Campbell (2001: 283-84).

spoken within the same community and so they come into close contact with each other, some members of the community will switch from one language to another (called 'code-switching'). "This code switching will lead to the mutual influence of those languages" (Culpeper 1997: 13).

Speakers of a language come into contact with speakers of another language(s) through travel or migration. People move to a foreign country to find a new life. For example, a lot of people around the world wish to migrate to the US these days. For that purpose, they should learn English before going there, and their study of English must continue even after the successful migration.[6] In this case, their mother tongue spoken in their homeland cannot but be influenced by English. The stronger the cultural and economic power of the contact foreign language is, the more easily the contacted language will be influenced. The contact language, e.g. English in the US, having so many immigrants, is also influenced by the language(s) of the upcoming people. That is, language change due to the language contact is mutual, although there may be more dominant language.[7]

The language contact can also be seen when a country was invaded by a foreign country. Such cases are seen in the earlier periods of English.[8]

---

[6] Languages might also change because people do not learn them perfectly. As people come into contact with others, they might learn the contact language imperfectly, which could ultimately cause the language to change.

[7] For example, California has so many Hispanic immigrants, so a lot of Spanish is spoken there. This situation surely influence English, too. Thus many Spanish words are becoming a part of English vocabulary. Of course, Spanish, at least spoken in North America, will also be influenced by English, adopting many English words and expressions.

Britain was invaded, e.g. by the Vikings at the end of the Old English period[9] and, a little later, by the Normans.[10] These two invasions left their

---

8) Although there are some minor disagreement for the division, the following is generally accepted as the chronological division of English (Fisiak 1995: 24-25, Barber 1993: 39):

Old English (OE)	Early OE	(c. 450 - 900)
	Late OE	(900 - 1100)
Middle English (ME)	Early ME	(1100 - 1300)
	Late ME	(1300 - 1500)
Modern English (ModE)	Early ModE	(1500 - 1650)
	Late ModE	(1650 - 1800)
Present-day English (PDE)	(1800 - Today)	

9) The Late OE period was the times of chaos caused by the Scandinavian invasions of England. These invasions, beginning in the later years of the 8th century, exerted a profound influence on all walks of life of the English people and at the same time on the English language, too. These Scandinavian invaders are generally called the Vikings. They were also Germanic peoples like Anglo-Saxons and they consisted of Swedes, Danes and Norwegians. They spoke the common language called Old Norse, from which Swedish, Danish and Norwegian are descended.

10) The **Norman conquest of England** (in Britain, often called the **Norman Conquest** or the **Conquest**) was the 11th-century invasion and occupation of England by Duke William II of Normandy, later styled William the Conqueror. William's claim to the English throne derived from his familial relationship with the childless Anglo-Saxon King Edward the Confessor. Edward died in January 1066 and was succeeded by his brother-in-law Harold Godwinson. The Norwegian king Harald Hardrada invaded northern England in September 1066 and was victorious at the Battle of Fulford, but Harold defeated and killed him at the Battle of Stamford Bridge on 25 September. Within days, William landed in southern England. Harold marched south to oppose him, leaving a significant portion of his army in the north. Harold's army confronted William's invaders on 14 October at the Battle of Hastings; William's force defeated Harold, who was killed in the engagement. ("Norman Conquest of England" In *Wikipedia*. Retrieved August 4, 2018)

vestiges, i.e. many Scandinavian and French loanwords in English. In the case of the language contact through the military invasion, the home language tends to be more strongly influenced by the language of the invader.[11]

Language contact is not the only language-external reason for language change. Its opposite, separation, also very often leads to language change. The example is the English language taken to America in the 17th century.[12] The American English, the English language spoken in North America is a little different from the one of its original homeland, i.e. Britain. Although there may be several reasons for this divergence, one reason is the physical separation between America and Britain, which caused a separate and independent development of each variety. Once in America, English changed in response to the new conditions that the settlers encountered, from physical geography to forms of government.[13] Furthermore, this was particularly the

---

11) It is hoped that this kind of forced language contact will not be possible any more.
12) The first expedition from England to the New World was sponsored by Walter Raleigh (?1552-1618) in 1584, and turned out a failure. The first permanent English settlement dates from 1607, when an expedition arrived in Chesapeake Bay. Thus the English language was brought to America in the same year by these English colonists (approximately 120 people). The colonists called their settlement Jamestown (after James I of the English king (1603-1625) at the time) and the area Virginia (after the 'Virgin Queen' Elizabeth I (1558-1603)). In November 1620 the Mayflower brought a group of pilgrims, later known as the Pilgrim Fathers, (102 in all, a group of Puritans which comprised 35 members of the English Separatist Church and the company of 67 other settlers). They set up the Plymouth Colony in the north in Cape Cod Bay. They had in common a new religious kingdom, free from persecution and 'purified' from the church practices they had experienced in England.
13) For example, British *Parliament*, consisting of *the House of Commons* and *the House*

case after political separation from Britain. Geographical separation, combined with the processes of language change, can often lead to regional differences (i.e. dialects).

Language-external causes of language change are also found even within a language community without any contact with a foreign language. One cause is the individual differences of language uses. That is, people do not always speak in the same way all of the time. Some people pronounce a certain sounds differently from others. And there is some difference at the vocabulary choice of individuals. We consciously or subconsciously take a liking to a particular word and use it with particular frequency and in a specific way. This individual variation provides the potential for change. It is particularly the case when the usage of some person is regarded as a marker of prestige. In this case other members of the speech community will, possibly subconsciously, begin to change their speech in the direction of prestige usage, in order to express their solidarity and identify with that person. Members of low and middle classes purposefully change their speech by imitating the elite of society in order to improve their own social standing. And, as a consequence, the upper class changes its language in order to maintain its distance from the masses. In social psychology, this quite natural process is called 'linguistic accommodation.' When this occurs on a one-to-one basis and is a temporary phenomenon, no language change results from it. But when such accommodation spreads from individual to individual and happens repeatedly over time, it can lead to language change.

---

of Lords, corresponds to American *Congress*, consisting of *the House of Representatives* and *the Senate*. This reflects the fact that America does not adopt the social rank system of Britain, which still has the nobility class (i.e. *lords*).

This 'accommodation' can occur even between regions. For example, the standard language, which is the language spoken in the capital area in most cases, is imitated and followed by the speakers of other areas. This kind of social change modifies speech.[14]

Language change caused by external factors is mostly clearly seen in the vocabulary. According to Culpeper (1997: 13-14), "The changes that have occurred in our physical environment, our culture, our social structures, our social attitudes and so on are often reflected in the language, particularly in the vocabulary and meaning". So many new words are created day by day.

1.2. Language-internal Causes for Language Change

We have so far discussed language-external conditions for language change. But there are language-internal reasons why language changes. In an academic sense these factors are more important because these factors are systematic, patterned and rule-governed to some degree.

There are so many examples of language-internally caused change. A prime example of this is the change of English from a synthetic or inflectional language, which relies on morphological endings to mark grammatical function, to an analytic one, which relies on word order for the same purpose. From a structural point of view, this is the most significant change that has occurred in the history of English. In Germanic languages the major stress generally falls on the word-initial syllable. OE,

---

[14] Thus, the proper understanding of language change also requires an analysis in terms of psycholinguistics and sociolinguistics.

as one of Germanic languages, had the same stress pattern. This meant that attention was drawn away from the end of the word, ultimately leading to the obscuring, and eventual loss of inflectional endings, which are added to the end of a word (more precisely, of a stem). This in turn caused English to become heavily reliant on word order to signal the basic grammatical relations such as subject, direct object, indirect object, etc. However, we do not know what caused the stress to fix on the word-initial syllable. It may indeed have been on account of some extralinguistic factor such as those we have discussed above, but we have no way of knowing this. Once the stress became fixed, anyway, it triggered this succession of internal changes.

The change of the English verb *do* from a full lexical verb to a so-called 'dummy' auxiliary verb after about 1500 is another example of system internal change. In this instance the original meaning was bleached out of the full verb *do*, and it became a lexically empty grammatical function word, used for example in yes-no questions (*Do you know the way home*?) and to support the negative particle *not* (*I don't smoke.*). We refer to this kind of system-internal change as grammaticalization. "Grammaticalization is generally seen as a process whereby a lexical item, with full referential meaning (i.e. an open-class element),15) develops grammatical meaning (i.e. it becomes

---

15) An open class (or open word class) is a word class that accepts the addition of new items, through such processes as compounding, derivation, coining, borrowing, etc. Typical open word classes are nouns, verbs, adjectives, (and adverbs). Closed-class words, on the other hand, are always relatively few and resistant to change. Prepositions, conjunctions, pronouns and interjections are all examples of closed-class words. For example, the Korean language has borrowed many English nouns (e.g. *mouse, computer, keyboard*, etc.) and verbs (e.g. *download, e-mail, fax,*

a closed-class element); this is accompanied by a reduction in or loss of phonetic substance, loss of syntactic independence and of lexical (referential) meaning" (Fischer and Rosenbach 2000: 2). English *will* was also a full lexical verb, meaning 'to want', but it was developed into the modern auxiliary verb, having grammatical meaning only, like the dummy *do*.

Grammaticalization is in many cases accompanied by reanalysis, where a word that historically has been associated with one particular structure becomes associated with another. The change of *do* from a lexical verb to an auxiliary is a kind of reanalysis, too. There are lots of examples of reanalysis in English. Another example is that English *naddre*, *napron* and *noumpere* have become *adder*, *apron* and *umpire* by reanalysis of the morpheme boundaries (i.e. [*a+naddre*] > [*an+adder*]). The converse has also happened; for example, the morpheme boundaries in the phrase *an ewt* have been reanalyzed to produce *a newt*. Reanalysis is an important reason for language change and it is a type of internal source of language change. But it is not clear what causes reanalysis itself. It is merely conjectured to be triggered by some other language-internal factor, not for a language-external reason.

Another cause of language-internal change is analogy. It means the application of one phenomenon to others by association. To take an example, an analogy can be the linguistic process that reduces word forms perceived as irregular by remaking them in the shape of more common forms that are governed by rules. For example, the English verb *help* once had the past (or preterite) *holp* and the past participle *holpen*. These

---

etc.), but not English prepositions and pronouns.

obsolete forms have been discarded and replaced by *helped* by the power of analogy (or by widened application of the productive Verb-*ed* rule.).[16] "A large proportion of analogical changes are morphological ones: they eliminate derivational opacity by generalizing transparent and regular patterns without, however, affecting the system of grammatical categories" (Bynon 1994: 110). However, irregular forms can sometimes be created by analogy; one example is the American English past tense form of *dive*: *dove*, formed on analogy with words such as *drive*: *drove*. Neologisms (i.e. newly coined words) can also be formed by analogy with existing words. A good example is *software*, formed by analogy with *hardware*; other analogous neologisms such as *firmware* and *vaporware* have followed. Another example is the humorous term *underwhelm*, formed by analogy with *overwhelm*. Such new words like *beefburger/eggburger* from *hamburger*, and *moonscape/townscape* from *landscape* are more examples. "Analogical changes are typically local rather than across-the-board: more often than not they operate within inflectional paradigms but not extend into the derivational morphology and quite generally they do not always take place when they could" (Bynon 1994: 110). And frequently used forms are resistant to analogical change. The irregular forms like *men, women, feet, oxen, children, wrote, hit,* etc. are all everyday words. So "frequency of occurrence is, clearly, a relevant factor in determining whether or not an analogical change will take place" (Bynon 1994: 110).

Another causal factor for language change is economy (the principle of

---

16) The analogical changes that reduce the number of relevant forms (technically called allomorphs) and make the paradigm more uniform are called *analogical levelling* or *analogical extension*. (Campbell 2001: 92-94)

minimum effort), which means that speakers of a language try to be economical in language use, generally towards 'ease of articulation'. So they adopt easy and simple expressions as much as possible, which can lead to language change. The desire for ease and simplification can lead to language change.

An extensive theory of language is needed to explain language change, and there are so many factors that influence each other. We should consider "internal factors, external factors, the structure of the language as a whole and how different part of the language interact with one another, the communicative and social functions of the language, the role of the individual, the role of society/the speech community, and more - that is the complex interaction and competition among a large number of factors" (Campbell 2001: 295). In spite of all these efforts, we cannot perfectly explain language change, since 'to explain (past) language change' means 'to predict the future of language', too. Nobody knows what will happen to us and to the languages we use in the future.

Chapter 02

Changes in Vocabulary: Lexical Change

One of the most conspicuous aspect of language change is the appearance of new words. It is inevitable to receive new words from foreign languages.[1] There are some 'language purists' who are trying to refuse and expel foreign elements from a language. However, borrowing of words is a natural process for any language to a large degree, just as language is bound to change.

Although some people are lamenting that English is 'killing' other languages, English itself has been influenced by a lot of foreign sources. We can see the evidence for that in the amount and variety of words poured into English. That is, new words have been pouring into English at a prodigious rate throughout its history, and the rate of introduction of new words is now perhaps greater than at any previous time. Language contact is mutual, which is easily evidenced in the exchange of words between languages. The borrowing of words can make the word stock of a language

---

1) For example, our language, Korean, is also provided with a lot of foreign words, especially from English these days.

rich. Besides the borrowing of words, there is another source to make a rich word stock. It is the creation of new words using its own material; word-coinage or word formation.

Getting new words (either through borrowing or through creating) is an important aspect of language change. The word inventory of a language changes according to the flow of time. An old word can just disappear, or can be replaced by the one imported from a foreign language, or can be transformed into a new one.

2.1. Borrowing Words from Foreign Sources

When speakers imitate a word from a foreign language and introduce it to their own language, the process is known as borrowing, and the word thus borrowed is called a loanword. Especially, the loanwords of English show its rather complicated history.[2] Therefore, the survey of English loanwords is important for the study of the history of English.[3]

OE, unlike PDE, was relatively inhospitable to the borrowing of foreign words. But at several points in its history it did accept some foreign words, principally Latin (through Christianity). Like Latin loanwords, borrowing from other languages, such as Celtic and Scandinavian languages (i.e. Old

---

2) The history of a loanword may be quite complex because such words have often passed through a series of languages before reaching English. *The Oxford English Dictionary* traces the ultimate etymology of every English word.
3) We will not give long lists of English loanwords such as we find in some textbooks like Pyles and Algeo (1993: Chapter 12). Instead, we will summarize briefly the cosmopolitan nature of PDE vocabulary.

Norse) also shows important cultural contacts.

In the ME period, the main sources of word borrowing were French and Latin. The general direction of French influence on English vocabulary was fairly clear after the Norman Conquest. A number of Latin words also came directly into English during the ME period. However, the great wave of Latin borrowing into English took place from the 15th century onwards, with the rise of Renaissance. And other sources, even non-Indo-European languages, also provided English with a lot of new words after the Renaissance, during the Industrial Revolution and the colonial period. Because of this long history of word borrowing, English has lost preeminently Germanic character.

2.1.1. Celtic

Celtics were the original languages spoken in the British Isles before the coming of the Germanic (ultimately, the English) people.[4] Despite the long occupation by the Romans, the British Celts continued to speak their own languages, though many of them, particularly those in the towns and cities who wanted to be "social climbers", learned to speak and write the language of their Roman rulers. These languages are descended into modern Celtic languages such as Welsh, Scottish Gaelic and Irish Gaelic.

Therefore, the English must have acquired some words from the Celts

---

[4] Before the English (mainly composed of such Germanic peoples as Angles, Saxons, Jutes, and possibly some Frisians) migrated from the Continent to Britain in the 5th century, the British Isles were already inhabited by non-Germanic peoples. That is, Celtic peoples had been there for a few centuries.

after their arrival. "Indeed the number of Celtic words taken into English in the whole of its history has been very small", however (Barber 1993: 101). The British Celts were a conquered people, and a conquering people are unlikely to adopt many words from those whom they have supplanted.

Probably there are no more than a dozen or so Celtic words introduced into English. Most of the words are place names and river names; *Kent* (C. *canto-* 'rim, border'), *Avon* (cf. *Stratford-upon-Avon*), *Dover* (C. *Dobrā* 'water') and *London* (C. *Londo* 'wild, bold'). And the element *-cumb* 'a deep, narrow valley' is also the Celtic element, as in *Duncombe* and *Holcombe*.

2.1.2. Scandinavian

The Late OE period was the times of chaos caused by the Scandinavian (Viking) invasions of England. These invasions, beginning in the later years of the 8th century, exerted a profound influence on all aspects of life of the English people, even on the English language itself.

However, although there were the enmity and the bloodshed between two peoples, there was also a feeling among the English that the Viking enemies are the same "family" as themselves. The Vikings were Germanic peoples like the Anglo-Saxons, so probably there was not much difficulty of communicating each other. Therefore, Scandinavian words could be easily introduced into English without much resistance. Many Scandinavian words closely resembled their English cognates because they belong to the same language family, i.e. Germanic.[5] Sometimes, they were so nearly identical that it would be impossible to tell whether a given word was Scandinavian or English. Sometimes, however, the meanings of obviously related words changed under the influence of the imported Scandinavian word. For example, *dream*, whose original English meaning was 'joy', acquired new meaning 'vision in sleep' under the influence of the related Scandinavian *draumr*.

An interesting thing to note here is that English words beginning in <sc-> with the pronunciation of [sk-] (some of which were later changed into <sk->) are mostly of Scandinavian origin. It is because Germanic [sk-] did not become palatalized in Old Norse as it did in OE, so that a word of Scandinavian origin will have [sk-] where one of English origin has [ʃ-]. The examples are such words as *scorch, score, scowl, scrape, scrub, skill, skin, skirt* (compare native *shirt*) and *sky*. Meanwhile, OE corresponding spelling <sc-> was pronounced as [ʃ-] and became to be respelled as <sh-> before the introduction of Scandinavian <sc-> or <sk-> words. But the <sk-> and <sh-> words had the same origin for each language. Thus *skirt* and *shirt* were originally the same words, meaning 'a short garment'; the former is Scandinavian and the latter is English.6) And *shrub* and *scrub* are the same.

---

5) English is west-Germanic, while the Scandinavians are all north-Germanic.
6) "Old English sometimes has [tʃ] where Old Norse retains [k], so that *church* is English and *kirk* Scandinavian, *ditch* English and *dike* Scandinavian. Again, Germanic [sk] did not become palatalized in Old Norse as it did Old English, so that a word of Scandinavian origin will have [sk] where one of English origin has [ʃ]: thus *shirt* is English and *skirt* Scandinavian (both words meaning originally 'a short garment'): and similarly with *shrub* and *scrub*." (Barber 1993: 130-31)

Table 2.1 Origins of *Sh-* and *Sk-* Words

Common Spelling	Origin	Later Development
sc-	OE [ʃ-] e.g. *scirt*	> *shirt*
	Scandinavian [sk-] e.g. *scirt*	> *skirt*

A fair number of words borrowed from the Scandinavian language closely resembled ones that already existed in OE, but they often had somewhat different pronunciations and meanings. These pairs of native and borrowed cognates are called doublets. The pair of <sh-> words and <sk-> ones is one example. Another examples are *no* (native OE) - *nay* (Scandinavian), *bench - bank, lend - loan,* and *whole - hale* (as in *hale and hearty*).

More important and more fundamental is what happened to the OE pronominal forms of the third person plural: all the <th-> forms, such as *they, their* and *them,* are of Scandinavian origin. Scandinavians had also provided English with the *-es* ending for the present indicative third person singular.[7] There was no -(e)s ending in OE, but instead an -(e)ð ending (-(e)ð > -(e)th > ø) was used. The old ending was gradually superceded by a new ending *-es* (> -(e)s) during the ME times.[8]

---

7) The same ending was used for the plural, too, for a long time, as in *wē, yē, thei bēres* 'we, you, they bear'.

8) Now the *-e-* is retained only after the hissing sounds like [s, z, ʃ, ʒ, tʃ, dʒ], as in *kisses, buzzes, brushes* and *coaches*. At first, however, the ending was invariable, i.e. always *-es*.

2.1.3. Latin

Latin is one of the languages which has exerted a profound influence on English and other European language as well. Although it is a dead language having no native speakers any more, its influence is still felt.[9] Latin is to western languages spoken in Europe what Chinese is to eastern languages such as Korean and Japanese. The influence of Latin is greatly important in understanding the features of English vocabulary, because English was dominated for a long time by such Romance languages as French and Latin (the ultimate ancestor of French). The introduction of Latin words into English has been accomplished roughly in five stages.

1) Latin Influence in the Germanic Period
Long before Anglo-Saxon speakers of English migrated to the British Isles, they had acquired a number of Latin word. These words are mostly concerned with military affairs, commerce, agriculture or with refinements of living. The Germanic peoples, including Anglo-Saxons, had a fairly close contact with the Romans since at least the beginning of the Christian era. There are about more than 150 early loanwords from Latin. Many of these words have survived into PDE. Examples are *ancor* 'anchor' (L. *ancora*), *butere* 'butter' (L. *būtyrum*), *cēse* 'cheese' (L. *cāseus*), *disc* 'dish' (L. *discus*), *mīl* 'mile' (L. *mīlia* 'a thousand [paces]'), *piper* 'pepper' (L. *piper*), *pund* 'pound' (L. *pondō* 'measure of weight') and *weall* 'wall' (L. *vallum*).

---

[9] Scholars, writers and businessmen still depend on Latin when they need invent new words and terms. For example, the Korean car name *Equus* is Latin, meaning 'horse'.

2) Latin Words through Celtic Languages

Before the coming of English peoples (Angles, Saxons and Jutes), Latin was spoken in the British Isles because the land was a part of Roman territory. So Latin words could penetrate into the languages of the British Celts, and then into English after the arrival of English peoples to the island. Examples of such Latin words are *candel* 'candle' (L. *candēla*), *ceaster* 'city' (L. *castra* 'camp'),[10] *cest* 'chest' (L. *cista*, later *cesta*), *mynster* 'monastery' (L. *monastērium*), *port* 'harbor' (L. *portus*) and *tīgle* 'tile' (L. *tēgula*).

3) Latin Words through Christianity

Even after the withdrawal of the Romans from the British Isles, Latin still had an influence on English, providing more new words. In particular, Latin words were again imported to English through Christianity (transmitted to England in AD 597 by St. Augustine's missionary).[11] Christianity was the official state religion of the Roman Empire after the emperor Theodosius (from AD 390)[12] and had a very strong power after

---

10) The English towns or cities ending in *-chester* or *-castor* 'city' (from Latin *castra* 'camp') were all the places for the military camps of the Roman troops.

11) **Christianity** played a very important cultural and political role in the OE period. "We know little about the Anglo-Saxons until after their conversion to Christianity, which introduced them to writing" (Barber 1993: 106). It came to Britain from two different directions: straight from Rome to Kent (When Gregory became Pope (Pope Gregory I the Great) in 590, he sent a band of missionaries comprising St. Augustine and forty monks to Kent in 596 in order to convert the Kentish king Æthelberht.) and from the Irish-Scottish monastery of Iona to the northwest.

12) **Flavius Theodosius** (January 11, 347 - January 17, 395), also called **Theodosius I** and **Theodosius the Great** was Roman Emperor from 379 to 395. Reuniting the

the fall of the Western Roman Empire in AD 476. The Bible was translated from its original languages (Hebrew and Greek) into Latin at that time.[13] To put it another way, Latin was the language of Christianity. The following words were all introduced into English through Christianity; *alter* 'altar' (L. *altar*), *apostol* 'apostle' (L. *apostolus*), *circul* 'circle' (L. *circulus*), *cristalla* 'crystal' (L. *crystallum*), *dēmon* (L. *daemon*), *fers* 'verse' (L. *versus*), *mæssse/messe* 'mass' (L. *missa*, later *messa*), *martir* 'martyr' (L. *martyr*) and *templ* 'temple' (L. *templum*). Of course, there are many non-religious Latin words imported in this OE period.

4) Latin Words Borrowed in ME Times

Many borrowings from Latin occurred during the ME period. Frequently, it is impossible to tell whether a word is from French or from Latin. It is because French was descended from Latin and so the two languages share a lot of the same words. Such words as *register*, *relation* and *rubric* might be from either language, judging by form alone. The word *port* may come from Latin *portus* 'harbor' / *porta* 'gate,' or French *porter* 'to carry'.

The Latin words borrowed into English in this period had to do with religion (e.g. *meditator*, *redeemer*, etc.), with law (e.g. *client*, *conviction*, etc.), with scholastic activities (e.g. *library*, *scribe*, *simile*, etc.), and with science (e.g. *dissolve*, *equal*, *essence*, *medicine*, *mercury*, *quadrant*, etc.).

---

eastern and western portions of the empire, Theodosius was the last emperor of both the Eastern and Western Roman Empire. After his death, the two parts split permanently. He is also known for making Nicene Christianity the official state religion of the Roman Empire. ("Theodosius" In *Wikipedia*. Retrieved July 31, 2018)

13) The Latin Bible here means **the Vulgate Bible** of the 4th century. It was translated into Latin by Jerome (c. 347 - September 30, 420).

There are much more.

5) Latin Words Borrowed in ModE Times

The great period of borrowings from Latin (and also from Greek, mainly by way of Latin) is the ModE period. There was a flood of Latin loanwords in this period, the peak being between about 1580 and 1660. The Renaissance of the 16th century generated interest in the past achievements of humanity, especially in ancient Greek and Latin literature, history and philosophy.[14] With this cultural movement, English adopted many new words from Latin and Greek, which were necessary in translating Latin and Greek writings into English.

The century or so after 1500 saw the introduction of, among many others, such words as *abdomen, area, compensate, data, editor, fictitious, folio, gradual, imitate, janitor, lapse, medium, notorious, orbit, peninsula, quota, series, strict, superintendent, transient, ultimate, urban* and *urge*.

PDE still uses Latin materials in coining new words.[15] Today's English

---

14) The arrival of **the Renaissance** (meaning literally 'rebirth' in French) from the Continent brought with it the revival of interest in human beings and their life. Together with this came the rediscovery and revitalization of the classical learning in Greek and Latin. Also, the fields of science, medicine and the arts were rapidly developed. The interest in ancient writings led to the translation of the works of Thucydides, Herodotus, Caesar, Tacitus, Plato, Aristotle, Cicero, Seneca, Homer, Virgil, Ovid, Horace, and many others.

15) "In this process, there was a strong tendency for writers to invent English technical terms by adapting those of the Latin originals, It must be added, however, that there was also a 'purist' movement (another manifestation of English nationalism) which attacked the use of loanwords, and advocated the coining of new technical terms native elements." (Barber 1993: 178)

does not import Latin words directly but coin new words using Latin morphemes. This will be the combination of borrowing and creating. For example, the international vocabulary of science draws heavily on such "neo-Latin" forms.

6) Latin Phrases and Abbreviations
Latin was the source of the following phrases and abbreviations:[16]

Table 2.2 Latin Phrases and Abbreviations

Category	Expressions	Meaning
Prepositional Phrases	*ad hoc*	for this (purpose)
	ad infinitum	to the unlimited, to infinity
	cum laude	with praise
	magna cum laude	with great praise
	summa cum laude	with highest praise
	de facto	from fact, in reality
	in situ	in (its own or its natural) place
	per capita	per head, per person
	per se	in or by itself
Noun Phrases	*modus vivendi*	way of living
	alma mater	nurturing mother
	prima facie	at first face, at first sight
Imperative	*carpe diem*	Seize the day!
Abbreviations	*c., ca., circum, circa*	about, approximately
	cf., confer	compare
	et al., et aliis	and others
	etc., etcetera	and other things
	e.g., exempli gratia	for sake of example
	ibid., ibidem	same place
	i.e., id est	that is, in other words
	op. cit., opere citato	(in the) work cited

16) The examples are all chosen from Denning and Leben (1995: 150-55).

2.1.4. Greek

There was no direct contact between English and Greek comparable to the close contact between English and French of the ME period. Nevertheless, English was strongly influenced by Greek. Greek was the original language of the Bible. Furthermore, it was the official language of the Roman Empire along with Latin, and at the same time the language of the Renaissance. So the influence of Greek on English was as strong as that of Latin. Many Greek words were introduced through the medium of Latin or French. For example, the word *church* was the Greek word transmitted to English through Latin. Other examples are as follows; *allegory, anemia, anesthesia, aristocracy, barbarous, chaos, comedy, cycle, dilemma, drama, electric, enthusiasm, epithet, epoch, history, homonym, metaphor, mystery, paradox, pharynx, phenomenon, rhapsody, rhythm, theory* and *zone*. The Greek words which were borrowed into English through French are *center, character, chronicle, democracy, diet, dragon, ecstasy, fantasy, harmony, lyre, machine, nymph, pause, rheum* and *tyrant*. But some words were imported straightly from Greek, like *acronym, agnostic, anthropoid, autocracy, idiosyncrasy, pathos, phone, telegram* and *xylophone*, among many others.

The borrowing from Latin and Greek provided another source for doublets in the level of affixes or roots as well as independent words:

Table 2.3 Doublets from Latin and Greek
(adapted from Denning and Leben (1995: 85))

Latin	Greek	Meaning
un(i)	*mono*	one
prim(e)	*proto*	first
di, du, bi	*dy, do*	two
second	*deuter*	second
tri, tris, ter	*tri, tris, trich*	three
quarter, quart, quadr	*tetra-*	four
quint	*pent(a)*	five
sex	*hex*	six
sept, speten	*hept*	seven
octo, octav	*octo-, okto-*	eight
noven, non	*ennea*	nine
dec, decem, deca	*deca, deka*	ten
cent	*hecto, hekto*	hundred
mille	*kile*	thousand
•	*mega*	million
•	*giga*	billion (10^9)
•	*tera*	trillion (10^{12})
plur, mult	*poly, myri*	many
tot	*omni, pan*	all
semi, demi	*hemi, hapl*	half
ambi	*amphi*	both

2.1.5. French

After the Norman Conquest in 1066, French became the official language in England. The influence of French on English was felt in every aspect of the English language. Even the great loss of inflections of English and the consequent simplification of English grammar were indirectly ascribed to the use of French in England. However, French influence is much more direct and noticeable upon the vocabulary. French words imported to English have to do with nearly all areas of life. The following are some example words of various fields.[17]

1) Government and Administration Words

The word *government* itself is French origin. It includes such words *crown, state, empire, realm, reign, royal, authority, majesty, court, parliament, rebel, noble, prince, duke, duchess. count, countess, baron,*[18] etc.

2) Ecclesiastical Words

In the religious sphere, many French words were borrowed into English, like *religion, abbot, clergy, preach, sermon, baptism, sacrament, creator, saint, savior, faith,* and many more. Such indications of rank or class as *clergy, prelate, cardinal, dean, parson, pastor, vicar, abbess, hermit* are again of French origin.

3) Law

French was the language of the law courts in England, so the greater part of the English legal vocabulary came from French, such as *justice,*

---

[17] Baugh and Cable (1993: §§ 123-30) give a detailed list of the loanwords of French origin.

[18] Words designating English titles of nobility, except for *king, queen, earl, lord* and *lady*, namely, *prince/princess, duke/duchess, marquise(marquess)/marchioness*[mɑ́:rʃəni], *count/coun tess, viscount/viscountess, baron/baroness* and *squire* are all of French origin. The English *earl* corresponds in rank with the French or continental *count*.

judg(e)ment, crime, suit, defendant, judge, attorney, jury, evidence, proof, verdict, sentence, prison and *gaol (jail)*.

Besides the above departments in which French altered the English vocabulary, there are much more examples relating to army, fashion, meals, social life, art, learning, medicine, and others. The adoption of French words was very general in every province of life and thought.

English has such doublets as *chattel/cattle, gage/wage, guard(ian)/ward(en), guarantee/warranty* and *jail/gaol*, for example. These doublets are due to the fact that French words have come into English from two dialects of French; Norman French (a northern dialect of French, later developed into Anglo-Norman in England) and Central French (that of Paris, later standard French). In the doublets exemplified above, the former forms such as *chattel, gage, guard(ian), guarantee* and *jail* are loanwords from Central French, while the latter forms like *cattle, wage, ward(en), warranty* and *gaol* are from Norman French. In Central French Latin <c> [k] before <a> developed into <ch> [č], but remained in the Norman dialect. Likewise, Old French <w> was retained in Norman French, but elsewhere, as in Central French, became [gw] and then [g].[19] "The spelling *gaol* (first recorded in 1163) is derived from Anglo-Norman *gaiole*, whereas the spelling *jail* (recorded in 1209) came from Central French *jaiole*" (Svartvik and Leech 2006: 35).[20]

It is interesting to note that the same French word may be borrowed at

---

[19] This is one of the processes which produced a lot of synonyms in English.
[20] "Today, the spelling *gaol* is an old-fashioned variant found in British English, but *jail* is preferred in dictionaries and is the standard spelling in North America." (Svartvik and Leech 2006: 35)

various periods in the history of English. Sometimes, the difference in the adopting time of the same word resulted in two different words in English. For example, *chief* (ME *chef*, from Old French, again from Latin *caput*, head) and *chef* (short for French *chef de cuisine* 'head of the kitchen') are both from the same origin. But the former form *chief* was imported into English in the 14th century, while *chef* was in the 19th. Between these two periods, French underwent a sound change where the Old French affricate [č=tʃ] was changed to the fricative [š=ʃ]. So the words with the [š=ʃ] pronunciation, like *chamois, chauffeur, chevron, chic, chiffon, chignon, douche* and *machine*, are later borrowing, while the [č=tʃ] words, like *chamber, champion, chance, change, chant, charge, chase, chaste, chattel, check* and *choice*, were borrowed in ME times.

2.1.6. From Other Languages

English has acquired a good many words from other languages, too. Such borrowing is still going on. Borrowing of words from foreign languages is mainly due to the contact of English-speaking people with foreigners through the exchanges in the form of trade, exploration or colonization. For example, English has a lot of words from Spanish, Italian, Dutch, German, and some words even from Arabic and Asian languages such as Chinese.[21] The example words will not be given here, but they are so naturalized into English that we cannot know which is a loanword from a foreign source and which is a native word. What is clear is that English has been willing

---

21) English has about 20 words imported from Korean, too.

to adopt foreign language sources. Such openness made English a language of international character.

2.1.7. Rich Synonyms in English

The richest foreign sources of English word stock are Latin, French and Greek, as we saw in the above. The richness of English in synonyms is largely due to this happy mingling of Latin, French, (Greek) and native elements. It has been said that English has a three-level synonym; popular - literary - learned.[22] Such a level distinction between synonyms can be exemplified in the word sets, as in the following:

Table 2.4 Three Level Synonyms of English[23]

Popular (from English)	Literary (from French)	Learned (from Latin)
rise	mount	ascend
ask	question	interrogate
goodness	virtue	probity
fast	firm	secure
fire	flame	conflagration
fear	terror	trepidation
holy	sacred	consecrated
time	age	epoch
kingly	royal	regal

---

22) In fact, there may be more levels in synonyms of English. This is the rough description.
23) The examples are from Baugh and Cable (1993: 186 §144) and Crystal (2002: 194).

In each of these sets the first is original English, the second is from French, and the third from Latin. The difference in tone between the English and the French words is often slight, whereas the Latin words are generally more bookish. However, it is more important to recognize the distinctive uses of each than to form prejudices in favor of one group above another.24)

In fact, there were some prejudices about the relative merits and demerits of Germanic and Romance (i.e. Latin and French) elements in the English vocabulary. The "Saxon" element (which is native to English) of the language was sometimes glorified as the strong, simple and direct component in contrast with many abstract and literary words derived from Latin and French. In such pairs as *deed - exploit, spell - enchantment, take - apprehend, weariness - lassitude*, the former native English words, which were rooted in OE, show superior directness, homely force and concreteness. But this account ignores the fact that there are a lot of simple and vivid words from French, too. The truth is that many of the most vivid and forceful words in English are French. Although the words of French and Latin origin are more literary or learned in many cases, this is just a tendency, not the rule. And it does not mean that such Romance elements are less or more valuable and important. Language has need for the simple, the polished, and even the recondite words.25)

---

24) "But more important than this, there are distinctions in the way the words are used. Thus we talk about *royal* blue, a *royal* flush and the *Royal* Navy, but a *regal* manner and a *regal* expression. There is no *Kingly* Navy or *Regal* Navy!" (Crystal 2002: 195)

25) The register and connotational differences are related to this "hybridisation of English vocabulary (*help/assistance, worsen/deteriorate, star/stellar, town/urban*, etc.)". (Rastall 2002: 30)

2.1.8. Borrowing and Morphological Irregularities

Borrowing of foreign words sometimes provides irregularities to English morphology. For example, the plurals are not formed by the addition of the ending -(e)s in many imported words, as follows:

Table 2.5 Irregular Morphology of Imported Words

Singular	Plural	Origin
crisis, oasis	*crises, oases*	Greek
criterion, phenomenon	*criteria, phenomena*	
datum, memorandum, symposium, millenium	*data, memoranda, symposia, millenia*	Latin
syllabus, alumnus	*syllabi, alumni*	
index	*indices*	
graffito	*graffiti*	Italian
cognoscente	*congoscenti*	

2.2. Creating Words from Native Sources[26]

Borrowing is not the only way to get new words. There is another way of expanding the vocabulary. It is to create new words from old materials (word formations or neologisms). English continues to form new words from existing resources. Affixing (or derivation) and compounding (or composition) remain the most important word formation processes.

---

[26] More detailed accounts for the word formation processes are given in the various textbooks for the Introduction to (English) Linguistics.

2.2.1. Nonce Formation

Sometimes, a new word can be created from nowhere. This process is sometimes called nonce-formation or root creation. Here, the words are completely original creations and have no 'roots'. This is not a common way to create a new word, but there are some examples. *Googol*, which means the word for the number 1 followed by a hundred zeros, is an example. Some rootless words are created to represent sounds. The word mimicking a sound is called an 'echoic' or 'onomatopoeic' word. *Cuckoo* is an classic example, and other examples are *bleep, honk, bang,* and others. Such words as *hobbit* and *triffid*, which were coined by Tolkien,[27] are another examples of root creation. Brand (trade) names are often made into common nouns, forming a special type of root creation (e.g. *coke, cola, coca-cola* from *Coca-Cola*; *frig* or *frigidaire* from *Frigidaire* (in the US), *kleenex* (tissue) from *Kleenex, levis* or *levi jeans* from *Levi Strauss, xerox* from *Xerox*).

2.2.2. Derivation

In spite of some words created through nonce-formation, the vast majority of words have some kind of etymology. That is, they have roots. There are several ways to get new words from the existing resources. Derivation or affixation, which is the adding affixes to form another word, is one such

---

27) **John Ronald Reuel Tolkien** (1892 - 1973) was an English philologist, writer and university professor, who is best known as the author of *The Hobbit* and *The Lord of the Rings*. He was an Oxford professor of Anglo-Saxon language (1925 to 1945) and English language and literature (1945 to 1959).

way. Affixes are short elements that usually do not exist as words in their own right but are attached onto a root word[28] in order to form another word (technically called 'bound morphemes').[29] Affixes that are placed at the beginning of a word are called prefixes (e.g. *un*pleasant, *de*plane, *mis*understand, *re*call, etc.) and affixes that are placed at the end of a root word are called suffixes (e.g. happi*ness*, material*ize*, sing*er*, mouth*ful*, etc.).[30] Affixes are mainly of two origins; one is English native (from OE), and the other is foreign. OE was well stocked with affixes, some of which are still commonly used. (e.g. happ*y*,[31] trul*y*, black*ness*, black*ish*, mind*less*, etc.). However, English affixes have expanded through the import of foreign ones. Just as English borrowed words, it also borrowed affixes.

2.2.3. Compounding

Another common way to create a new word is compounding or composition, which means the combining of more than two words to form another word. More accurately, it is the combination of more than two free morphemes. Compounds may have three different forms; open compounds

---

28) The **root** of a word is its most basic form, to which other parts, such as affixes, can be added. For example, the root of *sitting* is *sit*.
29) A **morpheme** means a minimal linguistic element having its own meaning. There are two kind of morphemes: bound morphemes (like the affixes) and free morphemes (independent words).
30) There are some rare cases where the root is not a free element but a bound one. For example, the *-ceive, -mit, -duce* are all roots, as we can see in the word sets like *re-ceive, con-ceive, per-ceive*, etc; *re-mit, per-mit, com-mit*, etc; *in-duce, re-duce, pro-duce*, etc. However, they cannot be used as independent words in English.
31) *Happy* is the combination of *hap* 'fortune' and the adjectival ending *-y*.

(e.g. *new born*), hyphenated compounds (e.g. *new-born*) and solid compounds (e.g. *newborn*). The older and shorter compounds are more likely to be solid, but it is a tendency.

The process of forming compounds by joining together two separate words which already exist was common even in OE. In fact, the richness in compounds is one of the noticeable features of Germanic languages. It is borne out in modern Germanic languages like Dutch and German.

Some very old compounds are hardly recognizable as the combination of two elements. For example, the word *lord* was originally the combination of two words, *hālf* 'loaf' and *weard* 'keeper, guardian'. The form *hālf-weard* was transformed into *hlāford*, and then into *lord*. This type is called specifically amalgamated compounds. Other examples are *sheriff* (<*scīr* 'shire'+*rēfa* 'reeve') and *daisy* (<*dæges-ēage* 'day's eye').[32]

2.2.4. Blending

Blending is the fusing of more than two words into an inseparable form. In blends, therefore, pieces of two (or more) different words are combined to create new words. In a sense, this is an extreme form of compounding. According to Campbell (2001: 104), "Usually the words which contribute the pieces that go into the make-up of the new word are semantically related in some way, sometimes as synonyms for things which have the same or a very similar meaning." Some classic examples are *smog* (< *smoke+fog*), *motel* (< *motor+hotel*), *brunch* (< *breakfast+lunch*), *splatter* (<

---

[32] You can get more examples in Pyles and Algeo (1993: 264-65).

splash+spatter), *flush* (< *flash+blush*), and more recent *bit* (< *binary+digit*), *webzine* (< *Website+magazine*), *videozine* (< *videotape+magazine*), *newscast* (< *news+broadcast*), *sportscast* (< *sports+broadcast*), *infomercial* (< *information +commercial*), and more. "Names of languages which borrow extensively from others or are highly influenced by others are the sources of such blends as *Spanglish* (< *Spanish+English*), *Finnglish* (< *Finnish+English*)" (Campbell 2001: 104-5). *Konglish* (< *Korean+English*), *Japlish* (< *Japanese +English*) and *Chinglish* (< *Chinese+English*) will be more examples.[33]

It may look very similar to amalgamated compounds. But the blends are the new words formed directly from the beginning, not losing its part as time flows. That is, blends occurs at the time the word is formed, and thus it is distinguished from a word like *lord* where fusion occurs over time.

2.2.5. Functional Shift

There are other ways in which a language enriches its lexicon. For example, there are many examples of functional/lexical shift or grammatical conversion. Functional shift is the using of one part of speech as another without using affixes.[34] For example, from the noun *parent* are derived the verb *parent* and its gerundial noun *parenting* 'performing the functions of a parent' as in *The midwife is very knowledgeable about parenting*. This method can add completely new words to the language with slightly

---

[33] Campbell (2001: 105) mentions syntactic blends as well as lexical blends. He says that for example, *I'm friends with him* is a blended form between *I'm a friend with him* and *we are friends*.

[34] So conversion is sometimes called 'zero derivation', too.

different nuances from existing words.

Almost any part of speech can be used as another. Even prepositions can be converted into nouns, as in *I'm coping with the ups and downs of life*. While many commentators deplore such usages, they nevertheless are widespread in English and signal living processes that will continue to enrich English and expand its lexical base.

2.2.6. Acronyms, Clipping and Back Formation

Another word-formational processes that are productive in the creation of neologisms are those of acronym and clipping. An acronym is the combining of the initial letters (or syllables in some cases) of words. There are so many examples, and new ones are created everyday; *TV* (< television)[35], *DIY* (< Do it yourself), *radar* (< radio detecting and ranging), *laser* (< light amplification by stimulated emission of radiation), *ASAP* (< as soon as possible), *Beemer* (< BMW automobile), *yuppie* (< young urban professions), *ZIP* (< Zone Improvement Program), and others. Such formations are frequently employed in the creation of names of corporations or institutions, as in *UNESCO* (< United Nations Educational Scientific and Cultural Organization).

Clipping is another way to make a short word, like acronyms. But the difference is that a clipped word is made by removing syllables of one word, not by combining materials from (more than) two words. That is, clipping involves the creation of a new shortened form of a word, which,

---

35) When an **acronym** is read alphabetically, not as an independent word, it is often referred to as an **alphabetism** or an **abbreviation**.

in most cases, supplants the original word. Thus the shortened word *bus* is used instead of the original full word *omnibus*. Other examples are *pants* (< *pantaloons*), *bra* (< *brassiere*), *ad* (< *advertizement*), *doc* (< *doctor*), *flu* (< *influenza*), *prof* (< *professor*), *condo* (< *condominium*), *fan* (< *fanatic*), *math*(*s*) (< *mathematics*), *limo* (< *limousine*), *nuke* (< *nuclear weapon*), to *perm* (< *permanent wave*), *psycho* (< *psychotic*), *pub* (< *public house*), and others. Very recent colloquial usages show such words as *zza* (< *pizza*), '*rents* (< *parents*) and '*hood* (< *neighborhood*).

Another special way to make a short word is back formation. It is substracting elements (often affixes) to form another word. For example, the word *editor* appeared before the word *edit*. Nevertheless, people mistakenly thought that the *-or* was the suffix meaning 'a person who is doing some work'. It is not the case; *editor* was a single morpheme which cannot be decomposed into *edit+or*. Here ignorance created something new. *Pea* (< *pease*) and *burgle* (< *burglar*) are the same. Another examples are *escalate* (< *escalator*), *letch* (< *lecher*), *orate* (< *orator*), *peddle* (< *peddler*) and *sculpt* (< *sculptor*).

2.2.7. From Proper Nouns

Another source of making a new lexical item is to use proper nouns as common nouns with relevant meaning changes. The words derived from proper names are called eponyms (cf. Fromkin, Rodman and Hymes (2003: 98)). Eponyms are one of the many creative ways that the vocabulary of a language expands.

Some words are from names of individuals or from names of groups of people. Examples are *guillotines* (named after the French physician *Joseph-Ignace Guillotin*), *sandwich* (named after *John Montagu, the 4th Earl of Sandwich (1718-92)*), *volt* (named after *Alessandro Volta*), *vandal/vandalism/vandalize* (from the *Vandals*), *gyp* 'cheat, swindle' (from *Gypsy*), *gothic* (from the *Goths*). Sometimes place names are sources of new words. Examples of this type are *denim* (from French' *serge* (a woolen fabric) *de Nîmes*), *peach* (from *Persia*), *jeans* (from *Genoa*), *currant* (from (*raisins of*) *Corinth*), *canary* (from *Canary Islands*), *spa* (from *Spa* (a place in Belgium)), *sherry* (from *Jerez* (a place in Spain)), *tangerine* (from *Tangier* (a place in Morocco)).

2.3. Current Changes in English Vocabulary

The expansion of English vocabulary is going on in great rate even in our time. A lot of new words are coined these days, too. In science and technology, many new words are coined from Greek and Latin morphemes, like *cosmonaut* and *stereophonic*. Barber (1993: 266-67) gives examples of new English words coined through affixation (e.g. <u>audio</u>visual, <u>mini</u>van, <u>neo</u>Nazi, <u>anti</u>-poll-tax, <u>de</u>bug, age<u>ism</u>, sex<u>ist</u>, skateboard<u>er</u>, etc.), through compounding (e.g. *spokesperson, JobCentres, resource center* 'a school library', etc.), and through shortening (e.g. *brill* (from *brilliant*), *vibes* (from *vibrations*)).

According to Culpeper (1997: 32), the sources of new vocabulary over the last fifty years are as follows:

Table 2.6 Sources of New Vocabulary in English

Compounding	36%
Affixation	27%
Functional Conversion	17%
Shortening (Acronyms, Clips, Back Formation)	9%
Blending	6%

Although loans are not a major source of new words these days, some loanwords are also found, like *disco(thèque)* (from French), *ombudsman* (from Swedish, Danish or Norwegian), *moped*[36] (from Swedish), *machismo*[37] (Mexican Spanish) and *anorak*[38] (from the Eskimos of Greenland).

In any case, new words are continuously entering into English, reflecting the fate of language to undergo the eternal change.

---

36) A *moped* is a lightweight motorized bicycle that can be pedaled as well as driven by a low-powered gasoline engine.
37) *Machismo* means a strong or exaggerated sense of masculinity stressing attributes such as physical courage, virility, domination of women and aggressiveness.
38) An *anorak* is a heavy jacket with a hood or a parka.

Chapter 03

Changes in Spelling and Pronunciation: Orthographic and Phonetic Change

The writing system of English is the alphabet, which was imported into English from Latin. It was clearly due to the strong political and cultural influence of the Roman Empire and, especially, to the propagation of Christianity. The Roman Alphabet is again based on the Greek alphabet,[1] which was again indebted to the Phoenician letters.[2] Before the

---

1) The original Roman Alphabet used the 23 letters. It was the same as PDE alphabet, except that there was no distinction between <i> and <j>, and <u> and <v>, and there was no <w>. The letters <j>, <v> and <w> were added in the ME period.

2) The history of the Roman alphabet is summarized as follows:

Egyptian hieroglyphs (at least for some letters) (c. 2000 BC) → A semitic alphabet (in Sinai) (c. 1750 BC) → Phoenician alphabet (based initially in today's Middle East) (c. 1000-800 BC) → Greek alphabet (based initially in today's Greece) (after 800 BC) → Etruscan alphabet (based initially in today's Italy) (c. 650 BC) → Roman alphabet (based initially based in today's Rome) (after 550 BC) (Culpeper and Archer 2009: 247)

introduction of the Latin alphabet, the Anglo-Saxons (or the Germanic peoples in general) had their own writing system that is called the Runes or the Futhorc. It is the collection of the angular letters.[3] But these letters remain in some inscriptions only and were not widely used. The letters should be angular for the easiness of inscribing on hard materials like stone, ivory or horn. Conversely, it was not suitable to write on the parchment. Irrespective of the usefulness of the Runes, they were immediately replaced by the Roman Alphabet, which was imported into nearly all the European languages. The problem is that the Roman Alphabet was not devised for the English language. It was just the borrowed writing system, so it did not have enough letters to represent all English sounds. Although the number of the alphabet letters used for English a little varies in each period of the development of English, it was much less for English sounds.

The present English alphabet contains twenty-six letters, whereas the language contains far more than twenty-six distinctive sounds. The number

---

[3] The **Runic alphabets** were used in northern Europe, in Scandinavia, present-day Germany and the British Isles. The alphabets are a set of related alphabets using letters (known as *runes*), formerly used to write Germanic languages before and shortly after the Christianization of Scandinavia and the British Isles. The Scandinavian variants are known as *Futhark* (or *Fuþark*, derived from their first six letters: *F, U, Þ, A, R* and *K*); the Anglo-Saxon variant as *Futhork* (or *Fuþorc*, due to sound changes undergone in OE by the same six letters). The common runic alphabet used throughout the area (i.e. *Futhark*) consisted of twenty-four letters, but the version found in Britain (i.e. *Futhork*) used extra letters to cope with the range of sounds found only in OE. At its most developed form, it consisted of thirty-one, sometimes thirty-three letters, as Table 4.4 shows. ("Runic Alphabet" In *Wikipedia*. Retrieved July 31, 2018)

of distinctive sounds (technically called the phonemes) are more than 40 (24-26 consonants and about 20 vowels).[4]

Table 3.1 English Alphabet

Letters for Consonants	b, c, d, f, g, h, j, k, l, m, n, p, q, r, s, t, v, x, z (19)
Letters for Vowels	a, e, i, o, u (5)
Letters for Vowel and Consonant together	y, w (2)[5]

In particular, English has about 20 vowel sounds, but only five vowel letters. Therefore, English had to invent new spelling conventions to represent all the sounds. This is the basic problem of the English spelling.

English spelling has other problems. For example, its pronunciations are not predictable in most cases. English spelling do not properly represent the pronunciation of the word. To put it another way, there is a big discrepancy between spelling and pronunciation. In other words, the PDE spellings are not fully regularized. This shows that the artificial efforts for the reforms of English spellings of the last centuries were not greatly successful and were not accepted widely by the public.

The English spelling system has a lot of peculiarities. English spelling

---

[4] For English phonemes and their proper phonetic features, see the textbooks for English phonetics.

[5] For example, <y> represents a vowel sound [i] when it appears after a vowel sound, as in *boy* [bɔi] and *clay* [klei]. When it appears before a vowel, however, it represents a consonantal sound, as in *yes* [jes] and *year* [jiər]. Some scholars prefer to use [y] instead of [i] or [j]; [bɔy] and [yes] instead of [bɔi] and [jes].

is not always phonetic. There is no simple one-to-one correspondence between sounds and the letters that represent them. Thus the same sound can be spelled so differently. For example, the [ei] sound are spelled so differently, as in *acorn/potato, hate/fate, day/pay, rain/pain, vein/veil, sleigh/weigh, they/grey, deign/reign, break/steak, métier/sauté, negligee, gauge, fete, gaol, eh*, and still others. Likewise, the [ʃ] sound are spelled in the 11 different ways, as in *shoe, nation, sugar, mansion, mission, suspicion, ocean, conscious, chaperon,*[6] *schist* and *fuchsia*. The [ou] sound has 10 different spellings, too, as in *so, sew, sow, oh, owe, dough, doe, beau, soak* and *soul*. Conversely, the same spelling can be pronounced so differently, as in *through* [-uː], *bough* [-au], *though* [-ou], *bought* [-ɔː-], *cough* [-ɑf, -ɔf], *rough* [-ʌf] and *hiccough* [-ʌp],[7] and others. Consider the sound difference between the two word groups in the following:

    heard vs. *beard*   *meat* vs. *great* vs *threat*
    moth vs. *mother*   *here* vs. *there*
    dear, fear vs. *bear, pear*   *dose, rose* vs. *lose*
    do vs. *go*   *dead* vs. *bead*
    word vs. *sword*, etc.

In the meantime, English has some words that are pronounced identically but spelled differently (called homonyms), such as *flower/flour, tale/tail* and *to/too/two*. On the other hand, there are such words as spelled identically

---

6) In French <ch> is pronounced as [ʃ], so English words having <ch> of [ʃ], like *chaperon, chef* and *chauffeur*, were in most cases borrowed from French.
7) This word is differently spelled as *hiccup*.

but pronounced differently; *lead* (the metal) / *lead* (the verb), *dove* (the bird) / *dove* (the past form of the verb *dive*), *bow* (a weapon for shooting arrows) / *bow* (to bend your head), *wind* (a current of air moving) / *wind* (the verb), and *bass* (the lowest range of musical notes) / *bass* (a type of fish).[8]

There are a lot of reasons for this chaotic situation.[9] The first and second reasons, which will be suggested below, are historical. First, the complication was observed from the beginning. As stated in the above, there were simply not enough letters to cope with all the OE pronunciations (nearly forty vowels and consonants), when English was first written down with the Roman Alphabet. The Latin alphabet used only 23 letters.[10] So some letters (e.g. <c> and <g>) were used to represent more than one sound, while some sounds were represented by the combinations of letters (e.g. <sc> for [ʃ] and <cg> for [dʒ]).

Secondly, as we will see below, English spelling and pronunciation have been changed since the OE times. In OE, the pronunciation of a word was

---

8) Technically, these words are called **heteronyms**. Two words are **heteronyms** if they are spelled the same, but pronounced differently, and have different meanings.
9) English spelling has been repeatedly condemned as 'chaotic', 'unpredictable', 'disorganized', 'a mess', etc. But it is not totally chaotic, as stated in Crystal (2002: 70, 72, 73).
 "English is much more regular in spelling than the traditional criticisms would have us believe. ... Accordingly, the suggestion that English spelling is fundamentally chaotic seems to be nonsense." (Crystal 2002: 72-73).
10) At first, the Romans had only 19 letters, <a, b, c, d, e f, h, i, k, l, m, n, o, p, q, r, s, t, u>. Later, they borrowed three additional letters from the Greek alphabet, <x, y, z>, and invented a new letter <g, G>, resembling <c, C>. Thus they finally had 23 letters.

transparent and rule-governed. So we can easily determine the sound only by seeing the spelling. After the Norman Conquest in 1066, however, English spellings began to be intermingled with foreign spelling conventions. A number of the apparent oddities of English spelling were introduced by ME scribes, particularly Norman scribes who adapted English spelling to suit French spelling conventions. The mixing of <u> and <v>, <i> and <j> are such examples. They also introduced new spellings into English: <qu> instead of OE <cw> (as in *queen*, cf. OE *cwēn*), <gh> instead of OE <h> (as in *night*, cf. OE *nīht*), <ch> instead of OE <c> (as in *church*, cf. OE *cirice*), and <ou> instead of OE <u> (as in *house*, cf. OE *hūs*). And later the early printers also introduced some oddities to English spellings, e.g. the use of <y> instead of <i>, the adding the superfluous <e> at the end of a word, and the doubling up of consonants. This foreign (mainly French) influence and the printing convention are another reason for the complexity of English spelling.

Thirdly, no single variety of English possessed the prestige of the standard English, and consequently every writer of English was inclined to use his or her own local variety and to spell it in whatever manner he or she liked. The result was that there was no single standardized spelling. In OE, ME and Early ModE there were no firm conventions for spelling.[11] In other words, in the pre-print era, when literacy was much less common, there was no fixed system with spelling. In the handwritten manuscripts that survive, words are spelt according to regional pronunciation and

---

11) It is said that Shakespeare himself wrote his names in several different ways (*Shagspere, Shackespere, Shake-speare* and *Shakespeare*), which means that even personal names (i.e. proper nouns) did not have a fixed spelling.

personal preference. Thus greater variation was tolerated than would be today. For example, the word *such* had so many different forms in ME, like *such, sich, sech, soch, swilk, swich, swech*, and much more.

The fourth and the most important reason is the fixing of English spelling and the continuous changes of pronunciation. The fixing of English spelling was mainly due to the introduction of printing in the 15th century and the consequent massive production of books, and to the influence of the dictionaries made in the 17th and 18th centuries.[12] Many people in the 16th century were highly critical of the tremendous variation in spelling, the addition of superfluous letters, and so on. From this time on, dictionaries started to appear which people could consult for an authoritative spelling. Coupled with printing, all this had the effect of fixing or standardizing spellings. In fact, the PDE spelling was only more or less fixed in the 18th century, when the great English dictionaries appeared. It is in this century that English spelling was standardized. The standardization of English spelling means that each word began to be

---

[12] The English language did not have a dictionary until the beginning of the 17th century. In the Middle Ages, difficult words were explained in English in marginal or interlinear notes in individual writings. Sometimes separate lists, not always arranged alphabetically, were appended at the end of texts. The first monolingual dictionary of English was published by Robert Cawdrey in 1604. Its title was *Table Alphabeticall (Alphabetical Table)*. This was a kind of 'dictionary of hard words', containing about 2,500 hard unusual English words borrowed from Greek, Latin, French and other languages. The next English dictionary was John Bullokar's *English Expositor* (1616), which contained more than 4,000 entries. Bullokar's dictionary was soon followed by Henry Cockeram's *English Dictionarie* (1623). Cockeram's dictionary as well as Bullokar's were reprinted several times. They were, however, still too small and should be expanded by other authors in the years to come.

spelled in one way. Dr. Samuel Johnson published a great dictionary in 1755. The influence of this dictionary was such that the spellings preferred by Dr. Johnson came to be accepted in almost every case as the standard spelling[13] and very few spellings have changed since his dictionary. Therefore, the PDE spelling represents the pronunciations of centuries ago, and not the present ones. For example, such words as *night*, *knife* and *sho<u>u</u>ld* reveal their old pronunciations, since the words did not have silent letters at all at the former times. In the meantime, pronunciation keeps on changing. The Great Vowel Shift is the representative sound change which occurred after the introduction of printing.[14] Ultimately, it becomes very important to trace the historical changes of English spelling and pronunciation to properly understand the chaotic relation between the two in PDE. So we go back to the OE period to see the initial state of English alphabetical system.

3.1. Spelling Change

The changes of English spelling were not so extreme, compared with those of pronunciation. Nevertheless, we can face some spelling differences. A few differences make the document written in OE or ME look like a foreign writing to PDE readers. So the understanding of some unfamiliar

---

13) In the US, however, it was not Johnson's dictionary but Noah Webster's dictionary of 1828 which largely settled American spelling. Thus such spelling contrast as *thea<u>tre</u>/theat<u>er</u>*, *col<u>our</u>/col<u>or</u>* and *analy<u>se</u>/analy<u>ze</u>* between the two national varieties of English began to arise.

14) The **Great Vowel Shift** will be explained later in this chapter.

spellings are very important in reading and understanding old documents. We should bear in mind that, when we read OE texts, every symbol must be pronounced in general and that even unstressed vowels must be given their full quality without being reduced to a schwa [ə].

3.1.1. Old English Spelling

- Letters for Vowel Sounds

The vowel letters in OE were <a, æ, e, i, o, u, y>.[15] So we can notice only two differences, compared with the PDE ones.

1) One is the use of <æ> as an alphabet letter, whose name is the *ash*. Now it is used as a phonetic symbol only. Instead of <æ>, <a> represents both [a: or ei] and [æ] together in PDE. But the pronunciation between [a: or ei] and [æ] is very confusing and not predictable, as in *far* [fa:r] and *fate* [feit] vs. *fat* [fæt]. In OE, however, <a> was always pronounced as [a], and <æ> always as [æ]. Actually, <æ> was the combination of <a> and <e>, so its capital letter was <Æ> (the combination of <A> and <E>). When the *ash* disappeared from English, the words which formerly had <æ> or <Æ> must be spelled either as <a/A> or as <e/E>. Thus *Ængles* was respelled as *Angles*, while *Ængla-land* and *Ængle-isc*[16] as *England* and *English*.

---

15) The symbol in < > is a spelling or a letter, whereas the one in [ ] is a sound or a pronunciation.
16) In OE [ʃ] was spelled as <sc>, not as <sh>, which is the later development.

2) The next difference is that <y> was always used as a vowel sound. Its phonetic value is [ü] (a front round vowel), not [i] (a front unround vowel). Such pronunciation is found in German but disappeared from English.[17]

3) Another difference is that all vowel letters represented either short or long sounds, vowel length being phonemically distinct. The long vowels had the macron (the horizontal mark (¯) used to indicate a stressed or long syllable) on it in some cases, not always. For example, *gōd*[18] was 'good', while *god* was 'god.'[19] Thus OE had 14 different vowel sounds: [a, æ, e, i, o, u, ü] and their long equivalents such as [a:, æ:, e:, i:, o:, u:, ü:].

4) The five vowel letters <a, e, i, o, u> symbolized what are sometimes referred to as "Continental" values - approximately those of Italian, Spanish, German, and to some extent of French as well. That is, <a, e, i, o, u> was always pronounced as [a, e, i, o, u], respectively. In other words, OE spelling was phonetic and so its pronunciation was fully predictable.

5) Some OE diphthongs were also represented by pairs of letters, which we call diagraphs.[20] For example, the diagraphs *ea* and *eo* were used,

---

17) In English all the front vowels are unround and all the round vowels like [u:, u, o, ɔ] are back vowels.
18) This pronunciation changed into [gu:d] in the Early ModE period due to the Great Vowel Shift, which will be dealt with below.
19) But *gōd* and *god* could be spelled as *god* indiscriminately.
20) A **diagraph** means the simultaneous use of two letters to represent a single sound.

58　The Internal History of English: Linguistic Changes

as in the OE words *eare* 'ear' and *beor* 'beer'.

- Letters for Consonant Sounds

The consonant letters in OE were <b, c, d, f, g, h, k, l, m, n, p, r, s, t, þ or ð, w, x, z>.

1) Some letters are missing in this entry. For example, the letters <j, q, v> were not used in writing OE. They were imported from French during the ME period. If you look at the English dictionary, you will notice that the lexical entries beginning with <j, q, v> are very small in number and that the words are mostly limited to French loanwords.

2) In the meantime, there is a letter which is not used any more; <þ> or <ð>. The name of <þ> is the *thorn* and that of <ð> is the *eth*. It was already mentioned above that English adopted the Latin alphabet, the alphabet for Latin. So the Roman Alphabet on its own was not enough in representing English sounds. Thus English had to invent new spellings or borrow some letters from other sources. The *thorn* <þ> was one of the Runes, while the *eth* <ð> was the spelling imported from Irish Gaelic. These two letters represented the sounds [θ] or [ð], so they are equal to the present diagraph <th>. But the two letters were used more or less interchangeably with each other. Thus

---

We have more examples like <-ng> [ŋ] as in *sing*, <ph> [f] as in *phone*, <ch> [tʃ] as in *church*, and others. Various vowel diagraphs are also used as in *conceive*, *deal*, and others. Using diagraphs is one way to compensate for the shortage of alphabet letters for English sounds.

both letters could indicate either [θ] or [ð]. The [ð] pronunciation was possible only between two vowels irrespective of the spellings. This means that [ð] was an allophonic variant of the phoneme /θ/.[21] For example, *brōðor* was pronounced as [brōðor], but it could be spelled as *brōþor* with the same pronunciation.

3) <w> could be spelled quite differently, i.e. as <Ƿ>, whose name is *wynn*. This letter was not from the Roman Alphabet but one of the Runes.[22] But this letter was replaced by <w> later.

4) The letters <k> and <z> [ts] were rarely used in OE.

5) <y> was always a vowel, as mentioned above.

6) The symbol <ȝ> could be used instead of <g>. It was an Irish form and <g> entered English writing later from the Continent.

7) OE used a few diagraphs for consonants, too. But the spellings of the diagraphs were a little different from present-day ones. For example, the diagraphs <cg> and <sc> were used to indicate the sounds, [ǰ or dʒ] and [š or ʃ], instead of <dg> and <sh>; for example, *ecg* 'edge,' *scīr* 'shire,' and *fisc* 'fish.'[23]

---

21) An **allophone** is one of several similar phones that belong to the same phoneme.
22) The original Roman Alphabet lacks the letter <w>.
23) Some phoneticians use the phonetic alphabets like [č, ǰ, š, ž] instead of the commoner [tʃ, dʒ, ʃ, ʒ].

8) The doubling of consonant symbols between vowels indicated length. Thus the <tt> of *sittan* 'to sit' indicated the double or long [t:] sound as in *hot tamale*, in contrast to the single consonant [t] in PDE *ho__tt__er*. Similarly <ll> in *fyllan* 'to fill' indicated the lengthened medial [l:], in contrast to the short [l] of present-day *fu__ll__y*.24) The <cc> in *racca* 'a cord, which forms part of the rigging of a ship' was a long [k:], as in *boo__kk__eeper*. Therefore, *ra__cc__a* was distinguished from *ra__c__a* 'a rake'.25)

9) Some letters, for example <c> and <g>, are ambiguous, since they can stand for more than one pronunciation. But most of the symbols are not ambiguous.

3.1.2. Middle English Spelling

OE spelling was generally phonetic and so did not contain silent letters. Why has English spelling system become less phonetic since then? Why is it now so complicated? The starting point of such complexity is the ME period.

During the ME period, English was strongly influenced by French, the language of the ruling class at the time. Just as French words were borrowed, so too were French spelling conventions. ME spelling was considerably more relaxed than present-day orthography.

---

24) Meanwhile, in PDE double-consonant symbols in two-syllable words are used to show that the preceding vowel is short, as in *wri__tt__en* and *co__pp__er*.
25) The two words merged into one spelling in PDE as *rake*[1] and *rake*[2].

▪ Letters for Vowel Sounds

1) To indicate vowel length, ME writing frequently employed double letters, particularly <ee> and <oo>.26) These particular doublings have survived into our own day, as in *feet* and *foot*. And other doublings, such as <ie, ei, oi, oy>, were also added in ME, together with OE <ea> and <eo>.

2) Final unstressed <e> following a single consonant, sometimes called "silent <e>", also indicated vowel length in ME, as in *fode* 'food', *fede* 'to feed', *case*, *bite* and *rule*. So this silent <e> cannot be deleted because it has the function of indicating vowel length.

3) Doubled consonants, which indicated consonant length in earlier periods, began in ME times to indicate that a preceding vowel was short. Surviving examples are *dinner* and *bitter*, in contrast with *diner* and *biter*.27)

4) The French spelling <ou> came to be used generally in the 14th century to represent English long <ū> - for example, *hous* (OE *hūs*)

---

26) These are equal to OE <ē> and <ō>.

27) There is a phonological rule where the final consonant should be doubled in affixing an ending -*ed* or -*ing* when the word ends in a short vowel and a single consonant. Such words as *digging/digged*, *cutting* and *omitting/omitted* are examples. Otherwise, the unaffixed forms would be misunderstood as **dige* (> **diging*), **cute* (> **cuting*) and **omite* (> **omiting*). This doubling is also a device to indicate the shortness of the preceding vowel. If the word contains a long vowel, the final consonant is kept single.

and *wo̲und* (OE *wūnd*).28) Sometimes <ow> was used instead of the expected <ou>, as in *do̲wn* (OE *dūn*), probably because of the confusability between <u> and <w> (i.e. double <u>).29)

5) <y> began to be used as a variant of <i>. Late in the ME period there was a tendency to write <y> for long <i>, as in *my̲* and *buy̲*, or for short <i>, as in *navy̲*. <y> was regularly used in final position and especially in environments where handwriting could be confusing (e.g. before or after <m, n, u, i>, cf. Footnote 28).

- **Letters for Consonant Sounds**

1) A few French spellings like <j, q, v> were imported. These letters were not used in OE. OE had the pronunciation of [v], but it was not spelled as <v>. Instead, the letter <f> represented [v] when it appears in an intervocalic position, as in *drifen* [dri̲ven]. But the letter <v> began to be used from this time. Thus the ME form of OE *drifen* was *dri̲ven* or *dri̲uen*. Practically all the words with initial <v> have been

---

28) For this reason, there is no <uu> spelling in PDE, but it was used for a short time during the ME period. The problem with double <u> was legibility. The characters <u>, <uu>, <i>, <n> and <m> were all written with straight down-strokes and were thus in danger of being confused, especially in the 'spiky' or 'angular' handwriting. To avoid this problem, scribes sometimes wrote <o> for <u> and <y> for <i>. Thus OE *su̲m/su̲nu/lu̲ve* were respelled as *so̲me/so̲n/lo̲ve*. Later, the pronunciation of the letter <ou> changed from its original sound [uː] to [au], due to the Great Vowel Shift, which will be explained later in this chapter.
29) <u> could be indiscriminately used instead of <v> for a long time in English. The interchange of <u> and <v> is still found to create a classic mood, as in MASSACHV̲SETTS INSTITV̲TE OF TECHNOLOGY.

taken from Latin or French. For example, such words as *vulgar* (Latin), *vocal* (Latin), *very* (French) and *voice* (French) were all imported, so they were once regarded as foreign words.

2) The imported <v> could be used instead of <u> from the ME period. <v> was the angular form of curved <u>, so both these two letters could indicate either consonant or vowel. It was the continental practice to use either symbol for either consonant or vowel. As a general thing, <v> was used initially and <u> elsewhere, regardless of the sound indicated, as in *very, vsury* (*usury*) and *euer* (*ever*). For this reason, we call the letter <w> 'double *u* (*uu*)', not 'double *v* (*vv*)'. This confusion might be related to the fact that the two letters are not easily distinguished in hand-written documents, as stated in Footnote 28.

3) Similarly, <uu> and a ligatured form as <w> could be used for [w] instead of the runic *wynn*.[30]

4) The diagraph <th> was introduced. As a matter of fact, this spelling was a return to earlier convention because it was used in some of the earliest English texts - those written before 900 - but was replaced in later OE writing by <þ> and <ð>. During the ME period, <th> was gradually reintroduced, and during Early ModE times its use was regularized.

5) ME employed a new spelling; <ȝ> (called *yogh*). This letter was used

---

30) <uu> is not used any more.

to indicate two sounds that came to be spelled <y> and <gh> later in the period.31) For example, *yield* and *knight* were written as *ʒeldan* and *cniʒt*, respectively.

6) <ch> was used by French scribes or by English ones under French influence to indicate the initial sound of *child*, i.e. [tʃ], which in OE had been spelled simply with <c>, as in *cild*. Until the adoption of <ch>, <c> had represented two phonemes: the first sounds of the words *chin* (OE *cin*) and *king* (OE *cyning*).32) Following a short vowel, the same sound might also be spelled <cch> or <chch>. Thus the present-day form *catch* could appear as *cache, cacche* or *cachche* at the time.

7) In Early OE times <sc> symbolized [sk], but, during the course of the OE period, the graphic sequence came to indicate [ʃ]. And the <sh> spelling was innovated to indicate this sound in the ME period by Anglo-Norman scribes (OE *sceal* - ME and ModE *shall*).

8) ME scribes preferred the inverted spelling <wh> for the phonetically more accurate <hw> used in OE times, like ME and ModE *what*, in contrast with OE *hwæt*.

9) French scribal practices are responsible for the ME spelling <qu>

---

31) For the complex history of this shape, the sounds they represented, and its relation with <g> and with the OE form <ʒ>, see the more detailed textbook for the history of English, like Pyles and Algeo (1993).
32) In other words, OE <c> could represent [tʃ] or [k], whereas it signals either [s] (before [e] or [i], as in *cell, city*) or [k] (elsewhere, as in *cool, cut*) now.

[kw], which French inherited from Latin, replacing OE <cw>, as in *quellen* 'to kill,' *queen* and *quethen* 'to say'[33]) (in OE *cwellan, cwen* and *cweðan*, respectively).

10) Also French in origin is the digraph <gg>, supplanting OE <cg> in medial and final position (OE *ecg* - ME *egge*), later written <dg(e)>, as in ModE *edge*.

11) The use of <gh> instead of <h>, as in *right* (OE *riht*), is also due to French influence.

3.1.3. Early Modern English Spelling

During the Early ModE period, English spelling conventions were gradually being fixed due to the introduction of printing. So the shapes of writing were gradually becoming similar to the present-day ones. However, a few differences deserve a short mention here.

- **Letters for Vowel Sounds**

1) <y> could be used instead of <i> after the Late ME period. This is not related to any sound change, but to the printers' convention. Printers used <y> instead of <i> because <y> took up more space.[34]

---

33) *quellen* 'to kill' and *quethen* 'to say' are obsolete now.
34) To produce a neat right-hand edge to a text, printers often added superfluous letters (often an extra <e>, or a doubling of the consonants of some words) and they also used <y> instead of <i>, because <y> took up more space on a given line.

This was done in order to increase the length of a line so that it would match the others of a text.35) All this added to the general variability in spelling.

- Letters for Consonant Sounds

1) The ME yogh <ȝ> was abandoned early in this period, being replaced by <y> and <gh>.

2) Early ModE also used <y> for the [ð] or [θ] pronunciation, along with <th> spelling. It was probably because the shape of <y>, especially in hand writings, resembles the OE spelling <þ>. Many of the early printers working in England were Dutch and they preferred to use continental letters. Thus non-Latin letters, such as the Runic *thorn* <þ>, were not well represented. Ultimately, the letter <y> of the similar form was chosen instead of <þ>. For example, y^e or y^t was used as an abbreviation for *the* (or *thee*36)) and *that*, respectively. ye was spelled as *ye*,37) too.

3) The present use of <i> for vowel and, <j> for consonant was not established until the 17th century. That is to say, <i> and <j> were

---

35) For the same reason, printers often added a superfluous <e> (e.g. *Olde*) and doubled up consonants (e.g. *Shoppe*).
36) *Thee* was the objective form of the old second person singular pronoun *thou*.
37) Thus the definite article could be spelled in the same way with the old nominative second person plural pronoun *ye*. A remnant of this can be seen in the sign *Ye Olde Tea Shoppe* 'The Old Tea Shop', where *Ye* is equivalent to *The*. Thus the abbreviation of the definite article *the* as *ye* survives to our own day.

interchangeable. It is comparable with the curved and angular forms of <u>, that is, <u> and <v>; they were used more or less indiscriminately for either vowel or consonant. In *King James Bible* (1611) and the First Folio of Shakespeare (1623), for instance, <i> is used for both values.

4) The sound indicated by <h> was lost in late Latin, and hence the symbol has no phonetic significance in those Latin-derived languages that retain it in their spelling (e.g. French). For this reason, <h> was regarded as a silent letter even in English. So <h> was inserted after <t> in a number of foreign words during the Renaissance. T*hrone*, t*heater* and t*hesis* were all such examples. They earlier had the initial <t> only. In addition, the English respelling ultimately gave rise to a change in the initial sound from [t] to [θ or ð].

5) Throughout most of the early ModE period, the 'long' <s>, with the shape of <ʃ> was used everywhere except at the end of a word, where only the 'short' <s> appeared. The 'long' <s> was abandoned in the 18th century.

3.2. Pronunciation Change

Like other aspects of language change, pronunciation also changes over time. English is not an exception. Over centuries, the pronunciation of English has changed at least as much as any other aspect of the language. Rather English is an example language which has undergone a radical sound change. The sound change continued even after the introduction of printing at the end of the 15th century, after which spellings were fixed to a great degree. It was already mentioned that this is one of the reasons that makes the discrepancy between sound and spelling in English. Especially, vowel sounds are generally unstable and permit variations between periods and between regions. English vowels, particularly long ones, underwent a radical change during its evolution.

However, the full treatment of English sound changes is beyond the description of this introductory book. So the basic and important changes are touched which are necessary to understand the PDE sounds and spellings.[38]

3.2.1. Old and Middle English Pronunciation

Our knowledge of the pronunciation of OE can be only approximate because we cannot determine the precise quality of any speech sound without tape recordings or its native speakers. Moreover, in OE times, as today, there were regional and individual differences, and doubtless social differences as well. But we can estimate the sound quality with high certainty by using various linguistic methods. The most important feature of OE pronunciation was phonetic. It means that the pronunciation was based on the spelling, so it was easily predictable. A certain spelling had a fixed and predictable value in any position. To put it differently, there was actually no discrepancy between sound and spelling.

So the seven OE vowel letters <a, æ, e, i, o, u, y> had the pronunciations

---

[38] For the full treatment of English spellings and their relations to the sounds, refer to Carney (1997)

of [a, æ, e, i, o, u, ü], respectively. And the corresponding long vowels were the same. That is, the vowels letters symbolized what are sometimes referred to as "Continental" values - approximately those of Italian, Spanish, German, and to some extent of French as well.

The consonant letters also had their own fixed phonetic value in most cases, although some letters could convey more than two phonetic values. For example, the letter <c> could represent two different sound depending on contiguous sounds. Preconsonantal <c> was always the velar stop [k], as in *cnāwan* 'to know' and *cræt* 'cart'. If <c> was next to a back vowel,[39] it also indicated [k], as in *corn* 'corn' and *bōc* 'book'. If it was next to a front vowel,[40] however, the sound indicated was the affricate [č or tʃ], as in *cild* 'child' and *cēosan* 'to choose'.[41] But the choice between [k] and [č or tʃ] was determined by its environment, so it is rule-governed and predictable.[42]

The pronunciation of <g> (usually written in a form more like <ʒ>) also depended on neighboring sounds. The symbol could indicate [y or j], along with the voiced velar stop [g]. The symbol indicates [g] before consonants

---

39) A **back vowel** is a vowel sound in which the tongue is positioned backward in the mouth, e.g. [u], [o] and [ɔ].
40) A **front vowel** is a vowel sound in which the tongue is positioned forward in the mouth, e.g. [i], [e] and [æ].
41) The spelling <c> of the value [č or tʃ] changed into <ch> in the ME period. So we have the forms like *child* and *choose* now. In the meantime, the <c> being adjacent to a front vowel has the [s] sound in PDE, as in *city*, *certain* and *cell*. But the preconsonantal <c> and the <c> next to a back vowel is still pronounced as [k], as in *cry*, *climate*, *cool* and *curtain*.
42) That is, <c> do not represent [s] in this position, unlike in PDE (e.g. *city*, *certain*, *cell*).

(e.g. *glæd* 'glad'), initially before back vowels (e.g. *gōs* 'goose'), and in the combination <ng> (e.g. *bringan* [briŋgan]). However, <g> was pronounced as [y or j], initially before the front vowel like <i>, <e> and <y> (e.g. *gēar* 'year'), medially between front vowels (e.g. *twēgen* 'twain' and *slægen* 'slain'), and after a front vowel at the end of a syllable (e.g. *legde* 'laid', *dæg* 'day' and *manig* 'many').43) But the choice between [g] and [y or j] were also allophonic and so predictable.44)

In OE, [v], [z] and [ð] were not phonemes; they occurred only between voiced sounds. So such words as *fōda* 'food' / *lof* 'praise', *sunu* 'son' / *mūs* 'mouse', *þorn* 'thorn' / *pæð* 'path' had voiceless fricatives, while the corresponding voiced fricatives [v], [z] and [ð] are found between voiced sounds, as in *cnafa* 'boy' / *hæfde* 'had', *lēosan* 'to lose' / *hūsl* 'holy', and *swiðe* 'very' / *broðor* 'brother'. So the choice between [f, s, θ] and [v, z, ð] was again rule-governed and predictable.

In conclusion, the sounds of English were phonetic in its initial stage, so we can predict the pronunciation of a word by looking at its spelling. And there was no silent letter at all in OE. But the regularity and transparency between spelling and sound broke down after the ME period.

During the ME period, the spelling of English changed by adopting new spellings, such as <w>, <ȝ>, <v>, <qu>, <wh> and <gg>, from French.45) Along with these new spellings, the sounds also changed in its own way.

---

43) The letter <g> of the value [y or j] was changed into <y> or <i> in the later times.
44) In some environments <g> also indicates the voiced velar fricative [ɣ], which sound disappeared from English.
45) For other ME spelling changes, refer to Section 3.1.2.

These independent developments of spellings and sounds in their respective way after the ME period began to trigger the discrepancy between spelling and pronunciation in English.

Although such tinkering with the orthography is one cause of the discrepancy between spelling and pronunciation in English, another and more important one is the change in the pronunciation of the long (or tense) vowels of English,[46] which is the most salient of all phonological developments in the history of English, This change is called the Great Vowel Shift, which occurred during the Early ModE period.

3.2.2. Discrepancy between Spelling and Pronunciation: Early Modern English Pronunciation

English suffers from irregularity and unpredictability between spelling and pronunciation. There are several reasons for this discrepancy. But the major reason is some sound changes which took place during the Early ModE period. The changes are mainly concerned with vowels, especially long vowels. However, we look at the situation of the short vowels before dealing with long vowels.

---

[46] An English tense vowel is generally pronounced as a long vowel, although the two terms are not the same phonetically. In General American tense vowels are used (e.g. [i] vs [ɪ]), while the corresponding sounds are pronounced as long vowels (e.g. [iː] vs [i]) in British Received Pronunciation. Here we will just use the term 'long' vowels from now on, disregarding such complicated phonetic issues.

3.2.2.1. Short Vowels

When we come to the vowel changes in Early ModE, we see the importance of the factors that determined the length of vowels in ME. All ME long vowels underwent extensive alteration in passing into ModE, but the short vowels, in accented syllables, remained comparatively stable. We can note only two changes of importance in the pronunciation of short vowels, those of <a> and <u>.

In Early ModE, the ME <a> had become an [æ] (e.g. c*a*t, th*a*nk, fl*a*x). In some cases this ME <a> represented an OE <æ>, e.g. *a*t, *a*pple, b*a*ck, since their OE spellings were *æt, æpple, bæck*. The new pronunciation was therefore a return to the OE pronunciation in this case. It is the usual pronunciation in America and a considerable part of southern England today. But there is still some regional and national variation between [a] and [æ] pronunciation.

Another vowel [u], which is a high back round vowel, was in many words unrounded into [ʌ], which is a mid central unround vowel. In ME this vowel was like the <u> in *full*. By the 16th century it became in most words the sound [ʌ], as in b*u*t, c*u*t and s*u*n.

Notwithstanding these two changes in short vowels, the PDE speakers will not have much difficulty in understanding the English of any period of the language, as far as short vowels are concerned. But the situation is quite different in the case of long vowels.

3.2.2.2. Long Vowels: The Great Vowel Shift

The situation is very different when we consider long vowels. During the ME period these long vowels also had the so-called "Continental" values. For example, <a> was pronounced like the [a:] in *father*.

During the Early ModE period, however, a great change is seen to be under way. All the long vowels, which had "Continental" values, i.e. Latin phonetic values previously, gradually came to be pronounced with a greater elevation of the tongue and closing of the mouth. So those five sounds like [a:, e:, ɛ:, o:, ɔ:] were raised one or two levels up, and those that could not be raised, i.e. the two highest long vowels [i:, u:], became diphthongs [ai, au], respectively.

This systematic change in the articulation of the ME long vowels during the Early ModE period is called the Great Vowel Shift. This shift had become general by the middle of the 18th century. The values of the long vowels form the main difference between the pronunciations of ME and ModE, and the Great Vowel Shift is one of the prominent historical events marking the separation of ME and ModE. The shift may be visualized in the following diagram:

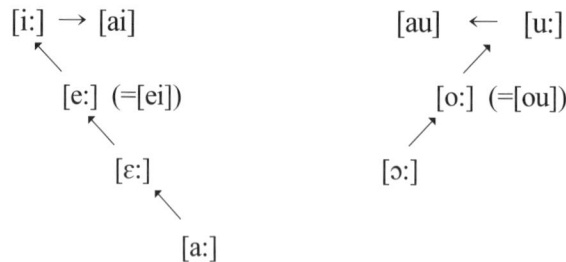

Figure 3.1 Diagram for the Great Vowel Shift[47)]

The changes indicated by the arrows must not be thought of as taking place successively, but rather as all parts of a general movement which took place roughly at the same time together. The principal changes are roughly as follows:

- ME [iː] was diphthongized to ModE [ai] (as in m*i*ce and f*i*ve).
- ME [uː] was diphthongized to ModE [au] (as in m*ou*se, h*ou*se and d*ow*n).
- ME [aː] was raised to [ɛː] and generally diphthongized in ModE to [ei] (as in m*a*ke and n*a*me).
- ME [oː] was raised to ModE [uː] (as in b*oo*t, t*oo*th and f*oo*t).
- ME [eː] was raised to ModE [iː] (as in f*ee*t, t*ee*th and m*ee*t).
- ME [ɛː] was raised to [eː] (=[ei]) and then to ModE [iː] (as in b*ea*k). In a few words beginning with consonant clusters, however, the vowel remained as [eː] (as in br*ea*k and st*ea*k).
- ME [ɔː] was raised to [oː] (=[ou]) (as in b*oa*t and c*oa*t).

The vowel in m*a*ke was originally pronounced similar to ModE f*a*ther (i.e. [a]); the vowel in f*ee*t was originally a long Latin-like "e" sound (i.e. [eː]); the vowel in m*i*ce was originally what the vowel in f*ee*t is now (i.e. [iː]); the vowel in b*oo*t was originally a long Latin-like "o" sound (i.e. [o: or ou]); and the vowel in m*ou*se was originally what the vowel in m*oo*se is now (i.e. [uː]).[48]

---

47) This diagram must be taken as only a very rough indication of what happened.
48) The effects of the shift were not entirely uniform, and differences in degree of vowel shifting can sometimes be detected in regional dialects both in written and spoken English. That is, exceptions occur, the transitions were not always complete, and

We can notice with ease that the Great Vowel Shift is greatly responsible for the discrepancy between vowel symbols and their sounds. The spelling of English had become fixed in a general way before the shift and therefore did not change when the quality of the long vowels changed. Consequently, vowel symbols no longer correspond to the sounds they once represented.

3.2.2.3. Weakening of Unaccented Vowels

Another vowel change is responsible for the discrepancy between sound and spelling. In unaccented syllables, the vowel spelling does not accurately represent the pronunciation today. This is because in all periods of English the vowels of unstressed syllables have had a tendency to weaken and then often to disappear. The weakening of unstressed vowels already began in the late Anglo-Saxon period and continued in ME.

For example, we do not distinguish in ordinary or rapid speech between the vowels at the beginning of *ago, upon* and *opinion*. The sound in all three words is [ə], which is called a schwa. The rule is that the unaccented vowels in English are commonly weakened to [ə] or [ɪ].[49] Consider the unstressed middle or final syllable in the words *intro̱dúce, élega̱nt, dráma̱, colo̱r, kingdo̱m* and *bréakfa̱st*. So the position of accent is crucial in determining the phonetic value of a vowel in English. For example, *úp* is pronounced as [ʌp], but the pronunciation of *upón* is different [əpá(ː)n or əpɔ́n]. The same morpheme *photograph* has different pronunciations according to the accent position in such words as *phótogràph* [fóutəgræ̀f]

---

there were sometimes accompanying changes in orthography

49) According to Smith (1994: 2489), [ɪ] spread from the north.

and *phòtogrúphic* [fòutəgrǽfik] vs. *photógraphy* [fətágrəfi / fətɔ́grəfi] and *photógrapher* [fətágrəfər / fətɔ́grəfər].

The collapsing of unaccented vowels into a schwa again made a distance between English spelling and sound. We must not be misled by the spelling.

3.3. Remedies for Discrepancy: Efforts for Spelling Reforms

The importance of the regularization of orthography, i.e. the accepted and correct way of spelling and writing words, already began to be stressed around the middle of the 16th century. It was to make the relation between spelling and sound more transparent and predictable. Until the 16th century English had no grammar books and dictionaries which could be consulted by students and teachers. Since then, however, the grammarians and orthoepists (scholars studying the correct spellings) made enormous efforts towards the standardization of English spelling, i.e. for spelling reforms. The earliest spelling reformers were Sir John Cheke and Sir Thomas Smith. They tried to make the English spelling phonetic, which means that all letters should be pronounced. Cheke proposed, among other things, to dispense with silent letters, to double vowel symbols in order to indicate length (as in modern Dutch or Flemish, e.g. *taak* for *take*, *maad* for *made*, etc.), and to use <y> for /θ/ and /ð/.

John Hart was another of the most important 16th century orthoepists. "According to Hart, the orthography of English is corrupt and suffers from four defects: diminution (too few symbols to represent the existing sounds), superfluity (the use of more letters than there are sounds in a given word, (i.e. silent letters like <b> in *doubt*), usurpation (the use of a wrong symbol or the use of the same letter for the different sound, like <g> in *gentle* [dʒéntl] and *give* [giv]) and misplacing (putting the letters in the wrong order, e.g. *fable* should be spelled *fabel* because its pronunciation is [féibəl]). To remedy the corruptions of English orthography of these kinds, Hart also proposed a number of changes. Among other things, he introduced a writing system in which one letter stands for one sound, diphthongs are rendered by diagraphs (e.g. *seid* for *side*), <j> represents /dʒ/, and others" (Fisiak 1995: 105-6). However, his proposals were not accepted by the public and failed to influence the development of English spelling in any significant manner.

A more conservative approach towards spelling reform was represented by Richard Mulcaster. Mulcaster was against any radical reform. He only wanted to correct details in English orthography. He argued for consistent usage based on tradition. According to him, English spelling was on the whole 'healthy' and required only minor operations. He dispensed with letters that had no functions (e.g. <t> in *putt* 'put'), regularized the use of final <-e> to indicate length in preceding vowels (e.g. *hope* vs. *hop, cane* vs. *can, shame* vs. *sham*), etc.[50] Mulcaster's work was very popular and contributed to the regularization of spelling. It is interesting to note that his spelling is close to that of PDE (cf. Fisiak 1995: 106).

In spite of many reformers' efforts and their some successes, the interest

---

50) The exception to this is the words ending in <-ve> such as *give, live, have*. Here the vowel is not long. The final <-e> was added just because no English word ends in <-v>. The only words ending in just <-v> are the clipped words like *gov* (<*government*), *lav* (<*lavatory*) and *Viv* (<*Vivian*).

in the reform of English spelling began to decline towards the end of the first half of the 17th century. But the interest in the reform of the English spelling system did not disappear completely. Even in the last 20th century a number of attempts have been made to simplify English spelling. The most famous campaigner for spelling reform was George Bernard Shaw.[51] However, spelling reform has so far failed to produce any changes in (British) English spelling,[52] although, in American English, spelling reform - promoted, in particular, by Noah Webster - has achieved a measure of success, leading such spellings as *theater* (from *theatre*), *color* (from *colour*) and *analyze* (from *analyse*).

According to Trask (2010: 149-52), there are a number of reasons why English spelling reform is unlikely. First, there exists a colossal amount of material written in English, so the spelling changes in many words can cause confusion in reading these materials. Second, we human beings are conservative creatures, so we are resistant to changing something, especially language matters. He says, by far the most important reason they cannot rationalize English spelling is that all the native speakers do not pronounce English in the same way, so there are no standards to follow in many cases. The conclusion is that it is too late to reform English spelling in any very sensible way.

---

51) **George Bernard Shaw** (1856 - 1950) was a British playwright and critic. He proposed his own English alphabet, called the **Shavian alphabet** (also known as **Shaw alphabet**).

52) "… The result is a system which, despite its weaknesses, has proved to be sufficiently functional that it has so far resisted all proposals for its fundamental reform." (Crystal 2002: 80)

Changes in Word Form: Morphological Change

Over the centuries, English has undergone an important shift in the way it signals grammatical information. In OE grammatical information was typically signalled by the inflectional endings of words. However, most of the endings were lost afterwards, and the loss of inflection caused consecutive changes in English morphology and grammar.

4.1. Inflection: Declension and Conjugation

One of the principal differences between OE and PDE is the complexity of the inflectional system shown in pronouns, articles/demonstratives, nouns, adjectives, adverbs and verbs. Only personal pronouns have preserved much of their ancient complexity.

Nearly all the Indo-European languages, including English, have bound morphemes that have a strictly grammatical function.[1] They mark properties such as tense, number, gender, case, and so forth. Such bound morphemes are called inflectional morphemes, or shortly inflections. English was a highly inflected language. Technically, a language is said to be a synthetic language when it has a lot of inflections. English was originally a synthetic language, since it heavily depended on inflections as signals of grammatical structure. However, it lost most of its inflections across time. At the present stage of English, there are a total of eight inflectional endings only; four in the verb, two in the noun, and two in the adjective (and adverb) (Fromkin, Rodman and Hymes 2003: 100-1):

Table 4.1 English Inflectional Morphemes and Their Examples

Verbal endings	-(e)s	third-person singular present	She wait-*s* at home.
	-ed	past tense	She wait-*ed* at home
	-ing	progressive	She is eat-*ing* a doughunt.
	-en	past participle	Mary has eat-*en* a doughunt.
Nominal endings	-(e)s	plural	She ate the donut-*s*.
	-'(s)	possessive	Jane'*s* hair is short. cf. Girls' school
Adjectival or Adverbial endings	-er	comparative	Jane has short-*er* hair than May
	-est	superlative	Jane has the short-*est* hair.

---

1) A **morpheme** is the minimal linguistic unit carrying its own meaning. Thus it is an arbitrary combination of a sound and a meaning that cannot be further analyzed. Every word in every language is composed of one or more morphemes. There are two kinds of morphemes. One is **free morphemes**, which may constitute words by themselves, like *boy*, *desire* and *gentle*. The other is **bound morphemes**, which are never words themselves but are always parts of words. There are again two bound morphemes; **affixes** (again **prefixes** like *un-*, *pre- bi-*, *mis-*, and a lot more, and **suffixes** like *-ness*, *-ity*, *-er*, and others) and **inflections**.

With the loss of many inflectional endings, PDE heavily depends on (a more fixed) word order and function words (like prepositions) to signal the grammatical structure. A language of this kind is called an analytical language.

OE nouns, pronouns and adjectives had four cases, which were used according to the function of the word in the sentence. Originally, Proto-Indo-European language had eight cases: nominative, genitive, dative, accusative, vocative, ablative, locative and instrumental. And these eight cases were well preserved in an ancient language like Sanskrit. But these eight cases were reduced just to four (or five) in OE: nominative, genitive, dative, accusative, and sometimes instrumental. Only adjectives, demonstratives and interrogative pronouns had instrumental case. Later, accusative and dative cases were collapsed into a single case, i.e. objective. Accusative case is for the (direct) object in general, while dative is for the indirect object only. So the merged objective case is still called accusative. At all events, PDE has three cases only; nominative (or subjective), genitive (or possessive) and accusative (or objective).[2]

As a matter of fact, there are two different types of inflection: declension and conjugation. Declension is the inflection of nouns, pronouns or adjectives for case, number, gender and person, and of adjectives also for

---

[2] Case reduction is still going on even in PDE. Although it is said that English has three cases, only six word pairs have the formal distinction between subjective and objective; *I/me, we/us, he/him, she/her, they/them* and *who/whom*. However, even these word pairs are losing case distinction. For example, *whom* is rarely used in an informal English, as we can see in such colloquial expressions as *Who (<Whom) did you see?* or *Who (<Whom) did you talk to?*

definiteness, since adjectives were inflected for definiteness as well as for case, number, gender and person. The weak declension of adjectives was used to indicate that the modified noun was definite, that is, when it named an object whose identity was known or expected or had already been mentioned.

It should be noted in relation to the notion of declension that OE had grammatical gender in contrast to the PDE natural gender system based on sex or sexlessness. The three genders of Indo-European were preserved in Germanic, and survived in English well into the ME period. The gender of a noun originally had nothing to do with sex, nor does it necessarily have sexual connotations. OE *wīf* 'wife, woman' is neuter, as is its German cognate *Weib*; so is *mægden* 'maiden,' like German *Mädchen*. *Bridd* 'young bird' is masculine; *bearn* 'son, bairn' is neuter. *Brū* 'eyebrow', *wamb* 'belly' and *eaxl* 'shoulder' are feminine. *Strengðu* 'strength' is feminine, and *drēam* 'joy' is masculine. However, the grammatical gender system collapsed during the ME times.

Another type of inflection is conjugation, which is the inflection of verbs for the categories of tense, person, number, mood and aspect. English, in common with other Germanic languages, divides its verbs into two groups according to how they form their past tense and past participle: 'weak (or regular)' and 'strong (or irregular)'. Weak verbs add a *-d* or *-t* to the root in order to form the past or the past participle (*talk - talked - talked*). So they are regular verbs in PDE.3) Strong verbs do not add an inflection, but

---

3) A few irregular verbs like *seek-sought-sought, buy-bought-bought, teach-taught-taught, think-thought-thought* and *bring-brought-brought* are also from weak verbs, since they end in a dental suffix.

change the root vowel (*drink - dr<u>a</u>nk - dr<u>u</u>nken*). The verbal inflections for the categories of tense, mood and aspect have been simplified over time, too, like (pro)nominal endings.

Case, number, gender, person and tense distinction is still maintained for nouns, pronouns, and verbs. But inflectional endings have been greatly reduced, and the grammatical gender system disappeared completely. Then, why did most of English inflections disappear? The loss of most inflections is argued to be due to two factors. One is the word initial accent of Germanic languages, to which OE also belongs. "During the Common Germanic period before OE and its sister languages began emerging as independent dialects, the word accent was shifted to the initial syllables of words, and this had a profound effect on the morphology of the subsequent Germanic languages" (Robinson 1994: 287). So OE words of more than one syllable, like those in all other Germanic languages, were regularly stressed on their first syllables. Due to the word initial heavy accent, the last (or ultimate) and the peultimate (i.e. the second to the last) syllables of words, which normally contain inflectional endings, were weakened or pronounced indistinctly. With the weak stress on the last syllable, the endings were not clearly distinguished each other, which led to the collapsing of <a>, <o> and <u> into a single sound, i.e. a schwa [ə] (spelled <-e> in most cases) in unstressed endings. The weakening continued after the levelling or merging of unstressed vowels into a schwa. So the levelled final [ə] was also gradually lost, leading to the general loss of inflectional endings.

The other conjectured reason is the mixing of OE with Old Norse. "Frequently the English and Scandinavian words were sufficiently similar to be recognizable, but had decidedly different sets of inflections. In these circumstances, doubt and confusion would arise about the correct form of ending to use, and speakers in bilingual situations would tend to rely on other grammatical devices where these lay to hand. The existence and growth of such other devices must itself have contributed to the decay of the inflectional system, while itself being stimulated by this decay" (Barber 1993: 157).

4.2. Pronouns

The first part of speech we will discuss is personal pronouns. Personal pronouns are the most highly inflected part of speech even in PDE, showing person (first, second and third), number (singular and plural) and case differences (subjective, possessive and objective). Personal pronouns still retain a considerable degree of morphological complexity that characterized them in OE. These words alone preserved distinctive subjective and objective case forms.[4] The paradigm for PDE personal (and possessive) pronouns is as follows:

---

[4] The exception is the neuter pronouns (*h*)*it* (and *that, this* and *what*), which even in OE had not differentiated the nominative and accusative. Another exception is the second person pronoun *you*, which has the same form for subject and object. This is due to the loss of the original subjective form *ge* (> *ye*) during the Early ModE period.

Table 4.2 Present-day Personal Pronoun Paradigm

			Subjective	Objective	Possessive	
					Determiner	Nominal
1P.		Sg.	*I*	*me*	*my*	*mine*
		Pl.	*we*	*us*	*our*	*ours*
2P.		Sg. / Pl.	*you*		*your*	*yours*
3P.	Sg.	Masc.	*he*	*him*	*his*	
		Fem.	*she*	*her*		*hers*
		Neu.	*it*		*its*	
		Pl.	*they*	*them*	*their*	*theirs*

The OE forms of personal pronouns were a little more complicated;5) for the first two persons are as follows:

---

5) In some respects, personal pronouns are more complex today. For example, PDE has the two genitive forms, e.g. *my/mine*. Previously, *min* could be used in the meanings of both 'my' and 'mine' together. *Thine* was the same.

i. *Myn* lord Chanselere come not here sone I come to Lundun (William Paston II, 1454; Paston, I, 155)

ii. and by many others how *thyne* owne credit made (Philip Gawdy, 1593; Gawdy, 78)

During the Early ModE period, *mine* and *thine* greatly receded, and by 1700 *my* and *thy* became the normal forms in standard English.

Table 4.3 Old English 1st and 2nd Person Pronouns

		Nom.	Gen.	Dat.	Acc.
1P.	Sg.	ic 'I'	mīn 'my, mine'	mē 'me'	mē 'me'
	Du.	wit 'we both'	uncer 'our(s) (both)'	unc 'us both'	unc 'us both'
	Pl.	wē 'we all'	ūre 'our(s) (all)'	ūs 'us all'	ūs 'us all'
2P.	Sg.	þū 'you (sg.)'	þīn 'your(s) (sg.)'	þē 'you (sg.)'	þē 'you (sg.)'
	Du.	git 'you both'	uncer 'your(s) (both)'	inc 'you both'	inc 'you both'
	Pl.	gē 'you all'	ēower 'your(s) (all)'	ēow 'you all'	ēow 'you all'

Besides the formal differences of individual pronouns, there were a few systematic differences between OE personal pronouns and PDE ones. First, OE had dual number pronouns. The dual number is found only in the first and the second person. The dual forms, which were used to talk about exactly two persons or two things, were disappearing even by the Late OE times. Secondly, the second person forms had the number distinction (þū 'you (sg.)' vs. gē 'you all (pl.)') in this period. Thirdly, The dative and accusative distinction was not alive,[6] and there was no gender distinction in the first and the second person. Gender appeared only in the third person singular form, as follows, like today's English:

---

[6] In other words, the first and the second person pronouns had the same forms for dative and accusative cases even in OE. This means that the merging of the two cases occurred for the first and the second person before the third.

Table 4.4 Old English 3rd Person Pronouns

		Nom.	Gen.	Dat.	Acc.
Sg.	Mas.	*hē* 'he'	*his* 'his'	*him* 'him'	*hine* 'him'
	Fem.	*hēo* 'she'	*hire* 'her(s)'	*hire* 'her'	*hī* 'her'
	Neu.	*hit* 'it'	*his* 'its'	*him* 'it'	*hit* 'it'
Pl.		*hī* 'they'	*hi(e)ra, he(o)ra* 'their(s)'1	*him, he(o)m* 'them'	*hī* 'them'

Note here that all the third person pronouns begin with <h>. That is to say, there were no <th-> plural forms like *they/them/their(s)*. *She* and *it(s)* were not used in OE. The <th-> forms are of Scandinavian origin, and they replaced the original <h-> forms completely during the Late OE and the Early ME times.[7]

PDE *she* has an unclear history, but it is perhaps a development of the demonstrative *sēo*, which will be discussed below, rather than of the personal pronoun *hēo*. A new form was needed because *hēo* became by regular sound change identical in pronunciation with the masculine *hē*, which is not an desirable state of affairs for language learners.

The masculine and feminine accusative forms *hine* and *hī*, and the neuter dative form *him* have not survived. The loss of <h-> in the neuter forms is due to lack of stress. The <h-> is often deleted in an unstressed situation, as in *Give her the book* and *Raise her up*.

Let us turn to ME forms. They are summarized as in the following table:

---

[7] The only remaining form is *'em*, which is the weakened form of OE *hem* with the usual loss of initial <h>. cf. *Call'em, Let me see'em*. It had variant spellings like *'em, em, am* and *um* in Early ModE. (Barber 1976: 207)

Table 4.5 Middle English Personal Pronouns

			Subjective	Possessive	Objective
1P.	Sg.		ich, I, ik	mi, min	me
	Pl.		we	our(e), oures	us
2P.	Sg.		thou	thi; thin	thee
	Pl.		ye	your(e), youres	you
3P.	Sg.	Masc.	he	his	him, hine
		Fem.	she, ho, hyo, hye, hi, scho, cho, he	hir(e), her(e), hires	hir(e), her(e), hi
		Neu.	hit, it	his	hit, it
	Pl.		hi, they, thai	her(e), heir(e), heres, theires	hem, heom, them, thaim, theim

The system of personal pronouns has undergone several major and a number of minor alterations from OE to ME. First, we can notice a lot of spelling variation. For instance, *she* had 7 more variants. Secondly, dative and accusative cases were collapsed into a single case, i.e. objective case. Thirdly, the dual forms disappeared completely. Fourthly, the <th-> plural forms could be used along with the old <h-> forms. Fifthly, because of such spelling changes as the change of <g> ([j or y] sound) into <y>, the replacement of <þ> by the diagraph <th>, the replacement of <ū> by <ou>, and the replacement of <ē> by <ee>, the second person pronouns could have new forms like *ye/your/you* and *thou/thi(n)/thee*.

Next, the Early ModE personal pronouns are shown in the following table:

Table 4.6 Early Modern English Personal Pronouns

			Subjective	Possessive	Objective
1P.	Sg.		*I*	*my, mine*	*me*
	Pl.		*we*	*our, ours*	*us*
2P.	Sg.		*thou*	*thy, thine*	*thee*
	Pl.		*ye/you*	*your, yours*	*you/ye*
3P.	Sg.	Masc.	*he, a*	*his*	*him*
		Fem.	*she*	*her*	*her*
		Neu.	*(h)it*	*his, it, its*	*(h)it*
	Pl.		*they*	*their, theirs*	*them, (h)em*

The system became much closer to the present-day one. *I* came to be capitalized in this period. It was from OE *ic* [itʃ], which was changed into *ich* (sometimes *ik* in the northern dialect),[8] and then into *I* because of the deletion of <-ch> [tʃ].[9] It was because the small letter *i* standing alone was likely to be overlooked. It is the most insignificant letter of the alphabet.

Still, a few differences are found. The number distinction of the second person singular pronouns was maintained at the early part of this period. But the singular <th-> forms, i.e. *thou* and its other forms, disappeared over time. The loss of the second person singular pronouns created a gap in the English pronoun system. That loss began with a shift in the use of the *thou* and the *ye* forms. As early as the late 13th century, the second person

---

8) In the northern England, <ch> was transcribed as a simple <k>, reflecting the local pronunciation of [k] instead of [tʃ]. So *church* was written as *kirk* and pronounced as [kərk] there.

9) The same deletion is found in the adverbial suffix *-ly*. The OE form of *-ly* was *līc*, a full noun that means 'body'. It was changed in ME into *lich* (as found in English place name *Lichfield*), and then weakened into *-ly* after the deletion of <ch>.

plural forms (*ye, you, your*) began to be used with singular meaning in circumstances of politeness or formality. In imitation of the French use of *tu* and *vous*, the English historical plural forms were used in addressing a superior, whether by virtue of social status or age, and in upper-class circles among equals. For this reason, the singular forms were regarded as impolite and sometimes rude, so people tried to avoid using the singular forms. The result was that the forms disappeared completely. The <th-> forms of the second person singular, which had become quite rare in upper-class speech by the 16th century, were completely lost on standard English in the 18th century, though they are still used in the dialects.

After the loss of the <th-> forms, English lost a useful way to distinguish the number for the second person. So it tried to devise new plural forms, like *youse, you-uns* (that is, *you ones*), *you-all* (or *y'all*), and the recent *you guys* 'you people'. But these forms are not regarded as standard, and not used widely.[10] From the later 17th century and throughout the 18th century, many speakers made a distinction between singular *you was* and plural *you were*, as in the following. But this distinction did not survive, either.

(1) Indeed, when *you was* in the irreligious way, I should not have been pleased with you. (*London Journal*: July 28, 1763)

In the second person plural, the old distinction between the nominative *ye* and the objective *you*, as in (2), was generally lost during the 16th century.

---

10) But these forms are still used in AmE (e.g. *you all* or *y'all* - in the South of the US, *yous(e)* in the Northeast of the US, especially New York City).

(2) The Lord deal kindly with *you*, as *ye* have dealt with the dead, and with me. The Lord grant *you* that *ye* may find rest. (The *King James Bible* [*Ruth* 1.8-9])

At first, the two forms were used for both subject and object discriminately, but in time the objective form drove out the subjective (at least in standard English).[11]

Another thing to note about the pronoun usage at this time was the formation of a new neuter possessive, *its*. As we saw in the above, the neuter pronoun declined as *hit*, *his*, *him* and *hit* in OE. But the dative *him* and the accusative *hit* were collapsed into a single objective *(h)it* by the general merging of the dative and accusative cases.[12] In unstressed positions *hit* weakened to *it*,[13] so at the beginning of the modern period *it* became the usual form for both subject and object.

His, however, remained the proper form of the possessive during the Early ModE period:

(3) a. But value dwels not in particular will, It holds *his* estimate and dignitie (Shakespeare, *Troilus and Cressida* II. 253-54)

---

11) The old subjective form is still used in some (British) dialects.
12) In most cases accusative case was merged into dative, as in *him* (< *hine*), *her* (< *hi*) and *(t)hem* (< *hi*). However, in the case of the neuter pronoun, the surviving one is the accusative form, *(h)it* (< *him*). This was quite clearly to prevent the confusion with the same form of the masculine objective form, *him*.
13) In Early ModE, *it* could be further weakened to *'t* and attached to the following or preceding auxiliary, as in *'tis* (< *it is*), *'twere* (< *it were*), *'twill* (< *it will*), *is't* (< *is it*) and *was't*. (< *was it*).

b. if the salt haue lost *his* sauour, wherewith shall it be salted
(The *King James Bible* [*Matthew* 13]).

Its occurrence where we should now use *its* is very common in written English down to the middle of the 17th century. But the possessive form *his* disappeared by reason of the confusion with the masculine possessive form, since both were formally identical. Instead, the uninflected *it* was used as the possessive form from the 14th to the 17th century:

(4) a. our english tongue hath crackt *it* credite (1581 George Pettie)
b. the hedge sparrow fed the Cookow so long, that it had *it* head bit off by *it* young (Shakespeare, *King Lear*).

But the simple possessive *it* also disappeared, although it is still used in some British dialects to this day. Other efforts to replace the ambiguous *his* as a possessive for *it* include paraphrases with *thereof*, as in (5a), and *of it*, as in (5b):

(5) a. on those of the ould faction, whom they suppose the authors *thereof* (John Helles, 1615; Holles, I. 76),
b. He had a letter to thee from me. I pray be mindful of the contents *of it* as soone as you can
(Thomas Knyvett, 1644; Knyvett, 144).

In the Early ModE period the third person singular masculine *he* could be reduced to *a* when it was not stressed, as follows:

(6) Now might I doe it, but now *a* is a-praying,[14)]

　　And now Ile doo't, and so *a* goes to heaven

　　(Shakespeare, *Hamlet* III. iii. 73-74).

In the third person plural the native <h-> forms had become all but archaic by the end of the 15th century and the <th-> forms, which were from Old Norse (the ancient Scandinavian (i.e. Viking) language), gradually took over the old forms. The only <h-> form to survive is '*em*, which is the unstressed form of the old *hem*, not of the later borrowed form, *them* (cf. Footnote 7).

Next, we will be concerned with interrogative pronouns. In OE *hwā* 'who' was declined only in the singular.[15)] *What* was the neuter form of *who*. The following table shows that the origins and later development of the interrogatives like *who/whose/whom, what* and *why*:

Table 4.7 Inflected Forms of *Who* and its Later Changes

	Masculine / Feminine	Neuter
Nom.	*hwā* > *whō* > *who*	*hwæt* > *what*
Gen.	*hwæs* > *whas* > *whos* > *whose*	*hwæs* > *whas* > *whos* > *whose*
Dat.	*hwǣm, hwām* > *whōm* > *whom*	*hwǣm, hwām* > *wham* > *whom* > ø
Acc.	*hwone* > ø	*hwæt* > *what*
Ins.	*hwǣm, hwām* > *whōm* > *whom*	*hwȳ* > *why*

---

14) For the <a-> before the present participle, see Sections 4.6 and 5.3.2.2.

15) There is no number distinction in the interrogative pronoun; <u>Who</u> *is she?* vs. <u>Who</u> *are all those people?* and <u>What</u> *is your book?* vs. <u>What</u> *are your books?* The singular form is used for plural meaning, too.

The OE masculine-feminine interrogative pronoun *hwā* became *whō* in ME (then *who*),[16] and the neuter form *hwæt* became *what*.[17] As with the other pronouns, the dative drove out the accusative (OE *hwone*). So the original dative *whom* (OE *hwām, hwǣm*) could be used in any objective function.

The neuter *hwæt* had the same dative form as *hwā*, i.e. *hwǣm, hwām* in OE. So the accusative form, *hwæt* (> *what*) survived as a single objective, instead of the confusing dative, *whom*, just as the accusative form of the neuter personal pronoun *(h)it* survived instead of the dative *him* to avoid the confusion with the masculine dative *him*. The genitive of both *hwā* and *hwæt* was *hwæs*. In ME this took by analogy the vowel of *whō* and *whōm*, thus *whōs* (then *whose*).[18]

Next, let us consider the development of relatives. In OE the pronoun *who* (*whom* and *whose*, too) was exclusively interrogative and so was not used as a relative at all. Instead, demonstratives, which will be discussed in the next section, were used as a relative, as in other Germanic languages:

(7) Syx dagas synd *on þæm* gebyrad þæt man wyrce
= Six days are *on which* is-fitting that one work
'There are six days on which it is fitting to work' (*St. Luke* 880)

In fact, the most frequently used relative pronoun in OE and ME is the

---

16) This is the result of the change of the OE long vowel <ā> ([a:]) into <o> ([o:] or [ou]) in ME, as in OE *stān* > ME *stone* and OE *hām* > ME *home*.
17) ME scribes preferred the inverted spelling <wh> for the phonetically more accurate <hw> used in OE times.
18) The final <-e> was added to indicate the length of the preceding vowel, and [hwo:z] was changed into [hwu:z] through the Great Vowel Shift.

indeclinable *that*:

(8) ða for he forð bi ðæm scræfe *ðæt* he oninnan wæs
 = then went he forth by the cave *that* he within was
 'then he passed by the cave that he was in' (*CP* 197.13)

It is still the case. In PDE *that* is used almost exclusively in restricted relative clauses, but it could be used in non-restricted contexts, too:

(9) Midas, *that* being chosen judge between Apollo ... and Pan, ... judged for plenty.
 (Bacon's *Advancement of Learning*; Barber (1993: 188)).

In the course of the 17th century, relative *that* became increasingly confined to restricted clauses.

OE had another indeclinable relative particle *þe*, as in (10), which was sometimes preceded by an appropriate form of the demonstrative *sē* to make a compound relative (11):

(10) & slea mon þa hond of *ðe* he hit mid gehyde
 and strike one the hand off *that* he it with did
 'and let one strike off the hand that he did it with'
 (*LawAf* I. 6 52)
(11) Eala ðu wundorlice rod *on ðære ðe* crist wolde ðrowian
 = Hail thou wonderful cross *on which that* Christ would suffer
 'Hail, thou wonderful cross, on which (that) Christ deigned to suffer'
 (*Alc.S.* 27.115)

But the constructions were lost after the ME times.

During the ME period *whō* was used only as an interrogative pronoun or an indefinite relative, meaning 'whoever', which occurred first in the 13th century:

(12) *Who* steals my purse steals trash.

The simple relative use of *who* was not widespread until the 16th century, though there are occasional instances of it as early as the late 13th century. The oblique forms *whōs* and *whōm*,[19] however, were used as relative in Late ME, at about the same time that another interrogative pronoun, *which* (OE *hwylc*), also began to be used as a relative. In other words, the oblique forms, *whom* and *whose*, began to be used as relatives before the nominative *who*.

At first, *which* could be used in reference to either persons or things, as in (13a). And *which* was sometimes followed by *that*, as in (13b). Or it could be preceded by *the,* as in (13c):

(13) a. The Mistris *which* I serue (Shakespeare, *The Tempest*).
   b. Criseyde, *which that* felt hire thus i-take.
      "Criseyde, who felt herself thus taken."[20]
      (Chaucer, *Troilus and Creseyde*)
   c. And Sir, I beseche your maistershipe to delyver to John Burton

---

19) An **oblique** case means non-nominative case.
20) In OE and ME the simple personal pronoun was used as a reflexive. On the development of English reflexive pronouns, refer to Lee (2007: Chapter 4).

the moneye *the which* is dewe to me

(Godard Oxbryge, 1478; Stonor, II. 49).

4.3. Articles and Demonstratives[21]

In PDE there are two kind of demonstratives: the proximal *this-these* and the distal *that-those*. And there is a separate definite article, *the*. There were two demonstratives in OE, too. The more frequently used was the *se*-demonstrative, which came to correspond in function to the definite article of today's English and so may be translated 'the' or 'that, those.' To put it differently, there was no independent definite article in OE. The other, less frequently used was the *þēs*-demonstrative, which is usually translated 'this, these'. Both demonstratives were inflected according to the number, case and gender of the modified noun. The inflected forms of the *se*-demonstrative were as follows:

Table 4.8 OE *Sē*-Demonstrative and its Later Changes

	Singular			Plural
	Masculine	Neuter	Feminine	
Nom.	sē, se > the	þæt > that	sēo > ø	þā > ø
Gen.	þæs > ø	þæs > ø	þǣre > ø	þāra > ø
Dat.	þǣm > ø	þǣm > ø	þǣre > ø	þǣm > ø
Acc.	þone > ø	þæt > that	þā > ø	þā > ø
Ins.	þȳ, þon, þē	þȳ, þon, þē > the	ø	ø

---

21) On the development of English articles and demonstratives, refer to Lee (1999a: Part II, Chapter 2).

Gender was distinguished only in the singular. The masculine and neuter forms were alike in the genitive, dative and instrumental. There was no distinct instrumental in the feminine or the plural. Because of the analogy of all the other forms, *se/sē* and *sēo* were in Late OE superseded by the variants *þe/þē* and *þēo*.

The PDE definite article *the* has developed from the masculine nominative *þe*, remodeled by analogy from *se*. When we use *the* in comparisons, however, as in <u>The</u> sooner, <u>the</u> better, it is a development of the neuter instrumental form *þē*, the literal sense being something like '<u>By this</u> [much] sooner, <u>by this</u> [much] better.'

The PDE demonstrative *that* is from the neuter nominative-accusative *þæt*, and its plural *those* has been borrowed from the other *þēs* demonstrative (from its nominative-accusative plural, *þās*), as we can see in Table 4.9. The *þēs* demonstrative, less frequently used OE demonstrative (usually translated 'this, these'), had the nominative singular forms *þēs* (masculine), *þis* (neuter) and *þēos* (feminine):

Table 4.9 OE *hēs*-Demonstrative and its Later Changes

	Singular			Plural
	Masculine	Neuter	Feminine	
Nom.	*þes*	*þis* > *this*	*þēos* > ø	*þās* > *those*
Gen.	*þisses* > ø	*þisses* > ø	*þisse* > ø	*þissa* > ø
Dat.	*þissum* > ø	*þissum* > ø	*þisse* > ø	*þissum* > ø
Acc.	*þisne* > ø	*þis* > *this*	*þās*	*þās* > *those*

The proximal demonstrative *this* was from the neuter singular nominative-accusative *þis*. By the 13th century, when gender distinction and some traces of inflection that had survived up to that time were lost, the singular nominative-accusative neuter *this* was used for all singular functions. The nominative-accusative plural *þās* developed into *those*. And a new plural was developed for *this*, namely *thise* or *these*, in ME. These developments have resulted in the *that-those* and *this-these* contrast. So demonstratives are inflected only in terms of the number, and the definite article is not inflected at all.

4.4. Nouns

OE had a large number of patterns for declining its nouns (called declensions). Only the most common types of declensions or those that have survived somehow in PDE are illustrated here.[22] Before that, we need to see the nominal pattern of PDE, which is summarized as follows:

Table 4.10 Present-day Noun Paradigm

	Singular	Plural
Sub. / Nom.	*the boy, the boss*	*the boys, the bosses*
Poss. / Gen.	*the boy's, the boss's*	*the boys', the bosses'*
Obj. / Acc.	*the boy, the boss*	*the boys, the bosses*

Present-day nouns have only two inflectional endings: -(*e*)*s* plural ending and -*'s* possessive ending.[23] But the OE nominal system was more

---

[22] To be exact, OE had four major and four minor noun declensions, which will not be discussed in detail here.

[23] The possessive ending loses <s> after the -(*e*)*s* plural form of a noun, as in *the boys'* and *the bosses'*.

complicated than this. If you look at Table 4.11 given below, there are five OE nouns listed: *hūnd* (> *hound*, 'any dog, not just a hound'), *dēor* (> *deer*, 'any animal, not just deer'),[24] *cīld* (> *child*), *oxa* (> *ox*) and *fōt* (> *foot*):

Table 4.11 Old English Noun Declensions[25]

Declensions		Masculine *a*-stem	Neuter *a*-stem	*z*-stem	*n*-stem	Root-Consonant Stem
Sg.	Nom.	hund	dēor	cild	oxa	fōt
	Gen.	hund*es*	dēor*es*	cild*es*	ox*an*	fōt*es*
	Dat.	hund*e*	dēor*e*	cild*e*	ox*an*	fēt
	Acc.	hund	dēor	cild	ox*an*	fōt
Pl.	Nom.	hund*as*	dēor	cild*ru*	ox*an*	fēt
	Gen.	hund*a*	dēor*a*	cild*ra*	ox*ana*	fōt*a*
	Dat.	hund*um*	dēor*um*	cild*um*	ox*um*	fōt*um*
	Acc.	hund*as*	dēor	cild*ru*	ox*an*	fēt

Each noun carries a set of different inflections that make up a declension for that noun. Specifically, we can see that there were several different ways of making a plural noun: affixing -*as* (> -*es* > -(*e*)*s*) ending (e.g. *hundas* > *hounds*), no inflection (e.g. *deer*), affixing -*r*(*u*) ending (e.g. *cildru* > *children*),[26] affixing -*an* (> -*en*) ending (e.g. *oxan* > *oxen*), and vowel change in the root (e.g. *fēt* > *feet*).[27] Only the first method is regarded as

---

24) For the meaning changes of the words *hound* and *deer*, see Chapter 6.
25) Here we can see a few distinctive endings. All nouns have the ending -*um* for the dative plural, and most have -*a* for the genitive plural, and many masculine nouns have a genitive singular in -*es* and a nominative and accusative plural in -*as*.
26) In fact, the -*ren* in *children* is the combination of two plural endings, -*re* (from -*ru*) + -*en* (from -*an*).
27) Vowel change *foot/feet* is a mark of the plural, but note that it is also found in

a regular and productive inflection for the plurality of a noun at present. The others are irregular. The number of the nouns that make their plural forms using these methods are very small in today's English:

Table 4.12 Irregular Plural Nouns in Present-day English

No inflection	*deer, sheep, swine, folk, kind*
Affixing -*r(u)* ending	*children*
Affixing -*an* ending	*oxen, children, brethren*[28]
Vowel change in the root (i.e. vowel mutation)	*feet, teeth, men, women, geese, mice, lice*

However, each of these methods was a 'regular' pattern in OE, and the number of nouns belonging to each declension was much larger than today. Among the various OE noun declensions,[29] however, the first one was the most important even in OE. More than half of all commonly used nouns were inflected according to this pattern, which was in time to be extended to practically all nouns. The handful of mutated-vowel plurals for the most part resisted this analogical tendency to be subsumed under the -*(e)s* plural, so that seven nouns listed above have survived to the present. A few more -*(e)n* plurals remained in Early ModE, for example, *eyen* 'eyes,' *shoon* 'shoes', *kine* 'cows', and a little more. The first two are now obsolete and *kine* continues to be used only as an archaic poetic word. *Brethren* also has

---

the dative singular and that not all plural forms had it. The vowel change in the root is termed **vowel mutation.**

28) *Brethren* is a double plural like *children* (*Childru*+*en*): vowel mutation + -*en* ending.
29) Each declension of Table 4.11 has its name. For example, the first one was called the *a*-stem declension, because [a] was the sound with which their stems ended in Proto-Germanic. But it will not be mentioned in detail here.

a very limited currency, confined to certain religious and fraternal groups. The uninflected plurals that survived to the present are also a few. Nowadays, new words invariably conform to what survives of the *a*-stem declension (cf. Footnote 29), for example, *hobbits, hobbit's, hobbits'*. So we may truly say it is the only living declension. The other patterns are all regarded as irregular and non-productive.

We said that the present-day general plural ending came from the OE masculine nominative-accusative plural (*-as* > *-es* > *-(e)s*) and the possessive singular was from the OE genitive singular of the same declension (*-es* > *-'s*). The forms of these two endings were different until very Late OE times. In ME times, however, both endings were spelled *-es* together, because the unstressed vowels had merged into a schwa [ə], spelled generally as <e>. Only in PDE have they again been differentiated in spelling by the use of the apostrophe.[30]

During the Early ModE period, special types of genitive constructions appeared. A remarkable construction is the use of *his, her* and *their* as signs of the genitive, as follows:

(14) a. Augustus *his* daughter 'Augustus's daughter'
       (E. K.'s gloss to Spenser's *Shepherds' Calendar*, 1579)
   b. Elizabeth Holland *her* howse 'Elizabeth Holland's house'
       (State Papers, 1546)
   c. the House of Lords *their* proceedings
       'the House of Lords' proceedings' (*Pepys's Diary*, 1667)

---

[30] The modern marks of punctuation were adopted after the introduction of printing. The comma replaced the virgule (i.e. /) in the 16th century, and in the 18th century the apostrophe became regular for marking noun possessives.

This use, called *his*-genitive, began in OE times but had its widest currency in the 16th and 17th centuries.31)

Another notable construction is the so-called group genitive:

(15) a. [King Priam of Troy]'s son
    b. [The Wife of Bath]'s Tale
    c. [the little boy that lives down the street]'s dog
    d. [the woman I live next door to]'s husband

This construction is a development of the Early ModE period. Though there were sporadic occurrences in ME, the usual older expression is illustrated by the following Chaucer's examples:

(16) a. the king Priam<u>us</u> sone of Troye cf. (15a)
    = the king Priam's son of Troy
    b. The Wyve<u>s</u> Tale of Bathe cf. (15b)
    = The Wife's Tale of Bath
    (or The Wyf of Bathe *Hire* Tale 'The Wife of Bath *Her* Tale').

As a consequence of the group genitive, the -'*s* possessive ending is now strikingly different from the other inflections, because it is added to (noun) phrases rather than to words. In this sense it has ceased to be an inflectional ending. It has instead become a grammatical particle that is pronounced as part of the preceding word (i.e. clitic),32) although it often goes syntactically

---

31) Many English speakers regard the historical genitive -'*s* as a variant of *his*.
32) A **clitic** is a grammatically independent and phonologically dependent word. It is

not with that word, but rather with a whole preceding phrase.

4.5. Adjectives and Adverbs

An OE adjective agrees with the noun it modifies. Germanic languages, in general, had developed this distinctive adjective paradigm of inflections. Adjectives were inflected according to its position as well as to the gender, case and number of the noun it modifies. So the OE adjective could have two different declensions; the weak and strong declensions. The weak declension was used after a demonstrative or a possessive pronoun, which made the following noun definite in its reference. On the other hand, the strong declension was used when the adjective was not preceded by a demonstrative or a possessive pronoun, or when it was predicative. The differences between the weak and strong declensions are shown through the following examples:

Table 4.13 Weak and Strong Declension of OE Adjectives

Gender of Noun	Weak Declension	Strong Declension
Masculine	*se dola cyning* 'the/that foolish king'	*dol cyning* '(a) foolish king'
Neuter	*þæt dole bearn* 'the/that foolish child'	*dol bearn* '(a) foolish child'
Feminine	*sēo dole ides* 'the/that foolish woman'	*dolu ides* '(a) foolish woman'

pronounced like an affix, but works at the phrase level. For example, the English possessive -'s is a clitic; in the phrase *the girl next door's cat*, -'s is phonologically attached to the preceding word *door* while grammatically combined with the phrase *the girl next door*, the possessor. ("Clitic" In *Wikipedia*. Retrieved July 31, 2018)

Fortunately to us, all the adjectival endings were lost completely after the OE times.

However, the inflections for the comparison of adjectives still remain. The comparative of adjectives was regularly formed by adding -ra, as in *heardra* 'harder', and the superlative by adding -ost, as in *heardost* 'hardest' in OE.[33] Due to the general levelling to <-e> of unstressed vowels in ME, the OE comparative ending -ra became -re, later -er, and the superlative suffixes -ost and -est (of Footnote 33) fell together as -est:

Table 4.14 Comparative and Superlative Endings of Adjectives

	Old English	after Middle English
Comparative	-ra	-re > -er
Superlative	-ost (-est)	-est

A very few others had kind of irregular comparative and superlative forms which have a different root from that of the positive (i.e. the base), as follows:

---

33) A few adjectives used the alternative suffixes *-ira, *-ist and consequently had i-mutated vowels. In recorded OE they took the endings -ra and -est but retained mutated vowels - for example, *eald* 'old' (> ME *old*), *yldra* (> ME *eldre* > *elder*) and *yldest* (> ME *eldest*). "I-mutation means the sound change whereby OE vowels harmonized to an /i/ or /j/ following them in the same word. This caused all back vowels to front and all short front vowels (except, naturally, /i/) and diphthongs to raise when an /i/ or /j/ followed in the next syllable." (Hogg 1992: 113)

Table 4.15 Irregular Comparative and Superlative Forms

Positive	Comparative	Superlative
gōd > *good*	*betra* > *bettre* > *better*	*betst* > *best*
micel 'much, many'	*māra* > *more*	*mǣst* > *most*
ēvel > *evil*	*worse*	*worst*
lītel > *little*	*lesse* or *lasse* > *lesser*	*lēste* > *least*

Next we will consider adverbs. The OE adverbial suffix was *-e*, not *-ly*; for example, *wrāð* 'angry', *wrāðe* 'angrily'. This *-e* was lost along with all other final *-e*'s by the end of the 14th century, with the result that many ModE adjectives and adverbs are identical in form; for instance, *loud, clear* (*I can hear you loud and clear.*), *deep* (*He thrust his hands deep into his pockets.*) and *slow* (*He drives too slow!*).34) Thus many adverbs that now must end in *-ly* did not require the suffix in Early ModE times. The works of Shakespeare furnish many examples: *grievous* (> *grievously*) *sick*, *indifferent* (> *indifferently*) *cold*, *wondrous* (> *wonderously*) *strange* and *passing* (> *surpassingly*) *fair*.

In addition, nouns and adjectives might be used adverbially, notably in the form of the genitive and the dative. The adverbial genitive is used, as in *He hwearf dæges ond nihtes*35) (*He wandered days and nights.*). Here *dæges and nihtes* is genitive, not plural historically.

The adverbial suffix *-ly* was introduced after the loss of the OE suffix *-e*. The suffix *-ly* was from the OE noun *līc*, meaning 'body', which was

---

34) Idiomatic meaning sometimes requires adverbial forms with *-ly*: *He plunged deep into the ocean* vs. *He thought deeply* (*extremely*) *about religious matters*, *Drive slow* vs. *He proceeded slowly*.

35) *Ond* was a variant of *and* in OE.

changed *lich* in ME. Then it became an affix of the form *-ly* because of the loss of *-ch* and the mixing use of <i> and <y>.36)

Adverbs regularly formed the comparative with *-or* and the superlative with *-ost* or *-est* (e.g. *wrāðor* 'more angrily' / *wrāðost* 'most angrily'). The *-or* ending was changed into *-er*, and the endings *-ost* and *-est* were collapsed into a single form *-est* in ME:

Table 4.16 Comparative and Superlative Endings of Adverbs

	Old English	Middle English
Comparative	*-or*	*-er*
Superlative	*-ost* (*-est*)	*-est*

Ultimately, adjectives and adverbs could have the same endings for comparison; comparatives with *-er* and superlatives with *-est*:

Adjectives and adverbs also used the so-called analytical comparison, which is the comparison with *more* (or *mo(e)*, a semantic equivalent of *more*) and *most* rather than *-er* and *-est*, the use of which forms makes synthetic comparison. The forms of *more* and *most* for comparison had occurred as early as OE times.

One thing to note is that the present stylistic objection to affixing the synthetic endings to polysyllables had somewhat less force in the previous stage of English. For example, in the Early ModE period the forms like *eminenter* (cf. *more eminent*), *impudentest* (cf. *most impudenest*) and *beautifullest* (cf. *most beautiful*) are found to be frequently used. Conversely,

---

36) As we have already mentioned in Footnote 9, this sound change is also seen in the development of the pronoun *I* (OE *ic* > ME *ich* > ModE *i* > PDE *I*).

monosyllablic words with *more* and *most* are also found, like *more near* (cf. *near<u>er</u>*), *more fast* (cf. *fast<u>er</u>*), *most poor* (cf. *poor<u>est</u>*) and *most foul* (cf. *foul<u>est</u>*). So the use of *-er* and *-est* endings and the use of *more* and *most* are in free variation without any restriction on its use. What is more, the use of the two methods at the same time, i.e. the so-called double comparison, was also possible in Early ModE:

(17) a. *more* larg*er* (Shakespeare, *Anthony and Cleopatra*)
 b. *more* near*er* (Shakespeare, *Hamlet*)
 c. There goest thou the *most* perfect*st* man that euer England bred a Gentleman. (Thomas Heywood, *A Woman Killed with Kindness*; Barber (1976: 202))
 d. This was the *most* vnkind*est* cut of all.
 (Shakespeare, *Julius Caesar;* Barber (1976: 202))

The general rule was that comparison could be made with *-er* and *-est* endings or with *more* and *most*, or, for emphasis, with both.

4.6. Verbs

As with nouns, verbs have experienced a dramatic loss of inflections. As shown in Table 4.1, PDE has only four verbal inflectional endings: *-e(s)* (third person singular present ending), *-ed* (past (or preterite) ending), *-en* (past participial ending) and *-ing* (present participial ending). In this section we will trace the origins of these four verbal endings.

Why do we add *-ed* to form the past tense of the verb *work* (*work<u>ed</u>*), whereas to form the past of the verb *write* we change the vowel (*wrote*)? It is because there were two completely different ways of making past forms of the verb in the OE times (more accurately, from the Proto-Germanic stage). English, in common with other Germanic languages, divides its verbs into two groups: weak and strong verbs. The verbs adding a dental suffix, that is, one containing -*d* or -*t* (immediately after voiceless consonants) to form their past and past participle are called weak verbs (as in present-day *talk-talked-talked*), while strong verbs changed their stressed vowel for the same purpose (as in present-day *drink-drank-drunken*).[37] The formation of past and past participles with a -*d* or -*t* is one of the defining features of Germanic languages differentiating from other Indo-European languages.

Most of the present-day irregular verbs are from OE strong verbs. OE had several different groups of strong verbs distinguished by their patterns of vowel change, so OE had a considerably larger number of strong verbs than PDE. The most important change to strong verbs is the conversion of a lot of strong verbs to weak ones. That is, there has been a tendency of irregular verbs to be regularized, through the analogy with regular verbs. So new regular forms such as *dived, hanged, weaved, strived* and *digged* could be used along with the old irregular ones like *dove, hung, wove, strove* and *dug*.

Besides the tense markings, verbs had their own peculiar inflectional endings to indicate person (first, second and third), number (singular and

---

[37] As we will see in Table 4.17, the past participle of a strong verb originally had the inflection -*en* at the end and also *ge-* at the beginning. So the OE past participle of the verb *drink* was *gedrunken*.

plural), mood (indicative, subjunctive and imperative) and aspect (progressive and perfective). The inflectional paradigm of verbs for the categories of tense, person, number, mood and aspect is termed conjugation. The conjugations of a typical weak verb, *cēpan* 'to keep', and a typical strong verb, *helpan* 'to help,' are as follows:[38]

Table 4.17 Conjugations of OE Weak and Strong Verb[39]

Present	1p.	*ic* (I)	*cēpe* 'I keep'	*helpe* 'I help'
	2p.	*þū* (thou)	*cēpest* 'you keep'	*hilpst* 'you help'
	3p.	*hē* (he), *hēo* (she), *hit* (it)	*cēpeð* 'he, she, it keeps'	*hilpð* 'he, she, it helps'
	Pl.	*wē* (we), *gē* (ye>you), *hī* (>they)	*cēpað* 'we, you, they keep'	*helpað* 'we, you, they help'
Past	1p.	*ic* (I)	*cēpte* 'I keep'	*healp* 'I helped'
	2p.	*þū* (thou)	*cēptest* 'you kept'	*hulpe* 'you helped'
	3p.	*hē* (he), *hēo* (she) *hit* (it)	*cēpte* 'he, she, it kept'	*healp* 'he, she, it helped'
	Pl.	*wē* (we), *gē* (ye>you), *hī* (>they)	*cēpton* 'I kept'	*hulpon* 'we, you, they helped'
Present Participle			*cēpende*	*helpende*
Past Participle			*gecēped*	*geholpen*

An important point to note is that, as with nouns, the general process

---

[38] *Keep* is now one of irregular verbs (*keep - kept - kept*). However, it was a weak verb in OE, because its past and past participle forms were made with the addition of a dental sound *-t*. So some of irregular verbs are from OE weak verbs. See Footnote 3. Meanwhile, *help*, which was a strong verb in OE, became regular later due to the analogy with other regular verbs.

[39] The full account of OE verbal endings is beyond this introductory textbook. So here are given indicative forms only.

over time has been one of simplification, i.e. the gradual erosion of inflections. English originally had a different and distinctive verbal ending for the first person singular (-*e* > ø), the second person singular (-(*e*)*st* > ø), and the third person singular (-(*e*)*ð* > -(*e*)*th* > ø), and the plural (-*að* > -*eth* > ø) in the present system. And the past tense of weak verbs had an inflectional ending for the second person singular (-*e*(*st*)). And the past plural also had the ending -*on*. However, all these endings disappeared over time. Now only the past tense of weak verbs (later regular verb) has the ending -*ed* (< -*te*). The strong (i.e. irregular) verb does not have any ending at all.

We can see that there was no present indicative third person singular -(*e*)*s* ending in OE. Instead, an -(*e*)*ð* ending (-(*e*)*ð* > -(*e*)*th* > ø) was used. The old ending was gradually superceded by a new ending -*es* (> -(*e*)*s*) during the ME times.[40] The new ending was from Scandinavian languages, like the third person plural pronouns *they/their/them*. That is, the Scandinavians (i.e. Vikings) who settled in the north had provided English with this -*es* ending.[41] Over time this ending spread southwards through the rest of England. The two endings could be used alternatively for a while during the ME times. By the Early ModE period, however, the -(*e*)*th* inflection was in serious decline, and came to seen as rather archaic. It survived longest in such words as *hath* (> *has*) and *doth* (> *does*), which

---

40) Now -*e*- is retained only after the hissing sounds like [s, z, ʃ, ʒ, tʃ, dʒ], as in *kisses*, *buzzes*, *brushes* and *coaches* (vs. *reads* and *writes*). At first, however, the ending was invariable, i.e. always -*es*.

41) The same ending was used for the plural, too, for a long time, as in *wē*, *yē*, *thei bēres* 'we, you, they bear'.

are still found in the 18th century.

Next, let us consider the origins of participial endings. The original ending of the present participle was -*ende*, which was replaced by a new ending -*ing(e)* during the ME times. The -*ing(e)* ending was from the OE verbal noun (or a gerund) ending -*ung*, like *leornung* 'learning, knowledge' (from *leornian* 'to learn') and *bodung* 'preaching, sermon' (from *bodian* 'to announce, preach'). This is the reason why PDE has the same ending for a verbal noun (e.g. *a sleeping bed* 'a bed for sleeping') and a present participle (e.g. *a sleeping baby* 'a baby who is sleeping').

Particularly, in the progressive, which consists of a form of *be* plus a present participle, the preposition *on* was placed in front of the present participle in earlier English. So the original form of a sentence like *She is reading a book* was something like *She is on reading a book* ('She is on the act of reading a book.'). To put it differently, the progressive construction was a kind of a gerundial construction historically. But the preposition *on* was weakened into *a-* (cf. (6)) and then disappeared completely without leaving any vestige.

The past participial endings, -*ed* for a regular verb and -*en* for a irregular verb, are all directly from the OE corresponding endings like *gecēped* and *geholpen*. The past participle prefix *ge-* was lost later, through the intermediate stage of the weakened form *y-* or *i-*.

There are a few anomalous verbs in terms of its morphology. For example, the verb *be* is a badly mixed-up verb, showing four different roots; *be/being/been*, whose infinitive in OE was *beon* (from Indo-European root **bheu-*), *are*/the obsolete form (*thou*) *art* (from Indo-European root **er-*), *am/is* (from Indo-European root **bheu-*), and the now completely dead forms like *sind/sint/sindon* (meaning "are", from Indo-European root **senti-*). The past forms like *was* and *were* were from yet another verb, whose infinitive in OE was *wesan*. Therefore, the verb *be* combined forms of what were originally four different verbs (excluding *sind/sint/sindon*). Paradigms which comprise historically unrelated forms, like *be*, are called suppletive (its nominal form is suppletion). Another suppletive verb is the *go-went* pair. *Go* was from the OE verb *gān*, whose past form was *eode*, whereas *went* was the past form of another verb *wend* (cf. *send-sent*). PDE lost *eode* but adopted *went* as a new suppletive past form for *go*.

However, some irregular verbs like *do-did* and *will-would* were not suppletive. *Did* was from OE *dyde*, the past form of *do* (its infinitive was *dōn*). *Would* was from OE *wolde*, the past form of *wille* (its infinitive was *willan*).

Chapter 05

Changes in Grammar: Syntactic Change

This chapter deals with syntactic changes of English sentences. Syntactic changes mean the changes in the grammatical structure of sentences. A sentence is composed of a subject[1] and a predicate.[2] The subject always contains a noun or something noun-like, whereas the predicate contains a verb. In terms of grammatical forms,[3] the subject constitutes a Noun Phrase

---

1) Sentences can be analyzed into subparts that we referred to as **constituents**. These constituents are termed "subject", "predicate", "object", "complement" or "adjunct", according to their **grammatical function,** i.e. how they function in the sentences of which they are a part.
2) The predicate is everything in the sentence except the subject.
3) The words of English (or languages in general) are grouped into word classes (also called parts of speech or syntactic categories) according to their **grammatical forms**, i.e. their formal features. The normal classification of English word classes are nouns, verbs, adjectives and adverbs (these are again grouped into **open class words**) vs. prepositions, conjunctions, determiners and interjections (these are grouped into **closed class words**). cf. Aarts (2001: 26). In the meantime, pronouns and auxiliaries may be postulated either as independent word classes or as special types of nouns and verbs, respectively.

(NP),4) whereas the predicate constitutes a Verb Phrase (VP). The predicate VP can contain an NP, an AP, a PP and/or other constituent as the object, complement or adjunct of the predicator.5) This basic structure of a sentence has not changed since the OE times. That is, OE syntax has an easily recognizable kinship with that of PDE. However, there are differences - and some striking ones, too. Nevertheless, they do not disguise the close similarity between OE sentences and their PDE counterparts. OE was English, too.

The full treatment of those differences is beyond this introductory textbook. We will just try to show how (and sometimes why) English sentential structure and its constituents have changed formally and functionally.

5.1. Word Order

We begin with the changes in word order in a sentence.6) OE word order is different from the order in PDE sentences, roughly in two respects. OE had the verb-final sentential structure, so its basic word order is arguably assumed to be Subject-Object-Verb (SOV). The verb-final order is easily observed in subordinate clauses:7)

---

4) A noun can be extended into a Noun Phrase, functioning its **head**. A VP, an AP, an AdvP and a PP are formed in the same manner. However, there is no DetP (Determiner Phrase), ConjP (Conjunction Phrase), and IntP (Interjection Phrase) in English.
5) A **predicator** is the grammatical function of a (main) verb.
6) For the detailed treatment of the word order changes in English, see Lee (1999a: Chapters 4-7), van Kemenade (1987), Pintzuk (1991), and the references cited there.

(1) a. þa ic ða þis eall *gemunde*

   = when I then this all *recall*

   'when I then recall all this' (*CP* 26)

   b. for ðæm ðe hie hiora nawiht *ongietan*

   = because they their nothing *understand*

   'because they understand nothing of them' (*CP* 30)

   c. gif hie ænigne feld *secan wolden*

   = if they any field *seek wanted-to*

   'if they wanted to seek out any open country'
   (*Parker* 894)

   d. ond se here þa burg *beseten hæfde*

   = and the army the town *besieged had*

   'and the (Viking) army had besieged the town'
   (*Parker* 894)

However, the verb-final order is not observed in most main clauses. Rather, the order seems to be the same with the PDE order, i.e. SVO, as the following example shows:

---

7) The other West Germanic languages such as Modern German (i and ii) and Dutch (iii and iv) show the verb-final pattern, too, as follows:

   i. daß Karl das Buch *kauft*
   = that Karl the book *buys*
   ii. daß Karl gestern das Buch *gekauft hat*
   = that Karl yesterday the book *bought has*
   iii. dat Karel het boek *koopt*
   = that Karel the book *buys*
   iv. dat Karel gisteren dat boek *gekocht heeft*
   = that Karel yesterday that book *bought has*

(2) Ælfric munac *gret* Æðelwærd ealdormann eadmodlice
 = Ælfric the-monk *greets* Æthelweard the-nobleman humbly.
 (*Parker* 1066)

But the superficial similarity breaks when we see the following sentences:

(3) a. eall þis *aredaþ* se reccere swiþe ryhte.
 = eall this *arranges* the ruler very rightly.
  'the ruler arranges all this very rightly' (*CP* 168.3)
  (accusative object first)
 b. Swelcum ingeþonce *gerist* þæt ...
 = Such-a disposition *suits* that ...
  'It is fitting for such a disposition that ...' (*CP* 60.10)
  (dative object first)
 c. þy ilcan geare *drehton* þa hergas on East englum ...
 = the same year *harried* the armies in East Anglia ...
  'in the same year the armies harried east Anglia ...' (*Parker* 895)
  (PP first)

In the examples given above, the verb is positioned just after the first constituent, whatever its grammatical function may be. Thus this pattern is called Verb-Second (V2).[8] A common analysis of the V2 structure is that

---

8) Modern German (and Dutch) also shows the V2 pattern, as follows:

 i. Karl *hat* gestern das Buch gekauft.
  = Karl *has* yesterday the book bought.
 ii. *Karl gestern das Buch gekauft *hat*.
  = Karl yesterday the book bought *has*.

the initial element is moved to a special position at the beginning of a sentence (a position for a topic-like element), and it somehow attracts the finite verb into a position to its immediate right (see van Kemenade (1987: 53, (79)) and Lee (1999a: 239, (28b)).

However, the frequency of SOV clauses, exemplified in (1), undergoes a slow but steady decline in the ME period. Although scholars like van Kememade (1987: 175) and Pintzuk (1991: 365-7) argue that the SOV pattern was changed into the modern SVO order around 1200, both patterns were used for a long time along with each other even after the 13th century. It indicates that the change in the basic word order progressed very slowly.[9] The reasons for the basic word order change have been conjectured and proposed in various ways. For example, Fischer and van der Wurff (2006: 187-188) mention such factors as language contact (i.e. the contact with the Scandinavian languages), heavy processing costs of embedded clauses in an SOV language (cf. This is the cat that the rat that the malt that in the house that Jack built lay ate killed.) and the loss of case distinctions. Anyway, the word order change caused changes in other syntactic constructions, too, a few examples of which will be mentioned below.

---

9) The fact that some examples of what was to become the regular order in later English, i.e. SVO, already existed even in OE subordinate clauses also shows the graduality of the relevant change:

i. þæt se winsele *wiðhæfde* heaþoderum
= that the wine-hall *withstood* brave-ones
  'that the wine-hall withstood the brave ones' (*Bo* 771-772)
ii. for þam þe hi *licettað* hie unscyldge
= because that they *pretend* themselves innocent
  'because they pretend themselves innocent'

A comparison with the PDE translation in (1)-(3) shows that the verb-final order and the V2 structure have basically disappeared from English. The V2 pattern disappeared from English around 1400 (cf. van Kemenade (1987: 183)), a little later than the assumed date of the basic word order change. The decline in the use of V2 was also gradual, so the inverted order is still found even in the Early ModE period:

(4) a. <u>Now</u> *comes in* the sweetest Morsell of the night. (Shakespeare, *Henry IV Part 2*; Barber (1976: 280))
   b. <u>Now</u> *would* I giue a thousand furlongs of Sea, for an Acre of barren ground. (Shakespeare, *The Tempest*; Barber (1976: 280))
   c. <u>In this place</u> *begins* that fruitful and plentiful Country which was call'd the vale of Esham. (1726 Daniel Defoe, *Tour of Great Britain* 441, 6; Fischer and van der Wurff (2006: 185))

This inverted pattern occurred in many situations where today the SVO pattern will be used, especially when the sentence begins with an adverb or adverbial phrase. Today, inversion is found only in a few cases. The representative case concerns clauses with an initial negative or restrictive element (e.g. *never, nor, only, rarely, seldom*, etc.) and with initial *there* or a locative phrase:

(5) a. <u>neither</u> *dyd* I suppose anny better sequele of it
      (Anthony Cave, 1551; Johnson, 1476)
   b. <u>nor</u> *have* such persons resorted to me
      (Edward Harley, 1665; Harle, 241)
   c. <u>Seldom</u> *have* I heard such nonsense.

d. <u>Not once</u> *did* he pause to consider ...

  e. <u>There</u> *goes* the last bus. (meaning "We've just missed it.")

Fischer and van der Wurff (2006: 184) also give some Early ModE examples, like the following:

  (6) a. <u>Seldom</u> *have* you seen anie Poet possessed with avarice
      (1594 Thomas Nash, *The Unfortunate Traveller* 44.25)
    b. <u>never</u> *will* I go abroad another fleet
      (1709 Declarivier Manley, *The New Atlantis* 10.2)

In general, instances of these patterns can be regarded as survivals of an earlier V2 stage of the English language.

The causes of the decline and the final loss of V2 in most contexts have been studied and mentioned broadly. For example, Fischer and van der Wurrf (2006: 185) point the factor of language contact (especially the influence from French and Scandinavian, where V2 is not observed). Another factors may be conjectured, too, but we will skip the detailed discussion of possible causes.

Along with the SOV base order and the V2 structure, OE also showed a relatively free word order. The freer order was possible, since OE was a heavily inflected language. In inflected languages, inflectional endings, rather than word order, show grammatical functions. "In OE we can say *sē cyning hæfde micel gefeaht* 'the king held a great council', and as a stylistic variant of this we can say *micel gefeaht hæfde sē cyning*, too. This is quite unambiguous, because the nominative article *sē* marks the subject of the sentence. The latter pattern just throws the emphasis on 'a great council'. In PDE, however, 'a great council had the king' has a different meaning from 'the king had a great council' (Barber 1993: 118). With the loss of inflections (and, of course, for other reasons, too) the word order of English became slowly fixed after the OE times".

5.2. Internal Structure of the Noun Phrase

Noun Phrases (NPs) can occur in various positions within the clausal unit depending on whether they function as subject, as object (direct or indirect), as complement, or as part of an adverbial or prepositional phrase. So the study of the internal structure of NPs is important to understand the general idea of how English grammar has changed. In fact, the change in the structure of NPs was not great, compared with that of VPs, which will be discussed in later sections.

The internal structure of an NP can be complicated, as follows:

Table 5.1 Internal Structure of the Noun Phrase

Determiners			Pre-modifiers	Head Noun[10]	Post-modifiers[11]
Pre-determiners	Central Determiners	Post-determiners			
all	her	many	good	**ideas**	*of the project*
what	a		marvellous	**suggestion**	*on the proposal*
	the	one	constructive	**proposal**	*to open another store*
	a few			**remarks**	*about the foods*
both	my father's			**parents**	

A determiner is a word that typically modifies a noun but has no descriptive content of its own. Such words 'determine' the referential and quantificational properties of the noun they modify. In general, three classes of determiners are distinguished on the basis of their position in an NP in relation to each other (Greenbaum and Quirk 1990: 72); Pre-determiners (e.g. *all, both, half, double* and *such*, as in <u>all</u> *the people,* <u>both</u> *her parents,* <u>half</u> *his front teeth,* <u>double</u> *that amount,* <u>such</u> *a period,* etc.), Central determiners (e.g. *the, a, this,* etc.) and Post-determiners. Central determiners have several subtypes; articles (*a(n), the*), possessive personal pronouns (*my, your, his, their,* etc.), demonstratives (*this/these, that/those*), interrogative adjectives (*which, what, whose* cf. (8d)), relative adjectives (*whose* cf. (8b), *which, whichever,* etc.) and indefinite adjectives (*some, any, no, every, each,* etc.). Post-determiners are cardinal numerals (e.g. *my* <u>three</u> *children,* etc.), ordinal numerals (e.g. *the* <u>first</u> *day, the* <u>last</u> *month,* etc.) and quantifiers (e.g. *seven, many, few,* etc. as in *the* <u>seven/many</u> *passengers, a* <u>few</u> *more times*).

Modifiers are adjectives in most cases, which do not deserve a lengthy mention here. So in this section we will briefly review some changes of noun heads and determiners only, leaving modifiers untouched.

5.2.1. Heads of the Noun Phrase

The essential element in an NP is its head, which can be either lexical

---

10) Only head nouns are obligatory in an NP.
11) Post-modifiers are again classified into simple modifiers (called adjuncts or adverbials) and complements (to a head noun). But we will not touch this complicated division here.

word (noun) or a grammatical word (pronoun). Personal pronouns and indefinite pronouns can function by themselves as heads, as in (7), while other pronouns, such as relatives, interrogatives and demonstratives, can be either head or determiner of a nominal head, as in (8):

(7) a. *He* was the perfect gentleman.
   b. *Somebody* should have told me.
(8) a. The person, *who* we had been talking about earlier, walked in.
   b. It's the house *whose* door's painted red.
   c. *Who*'s money for?
   d. *Whose* house is that?
   e. *That*'s Peter over there.
   f. Look at *that* man over there.

In some cases, however, a personal pronoun can be modified by another element, like *poor old me*, *us girls* and *he in the corner* (Denison 1998: 106ff.). "In such usages, they are in fact similar to referential nouns" (Fischer and van der Wurff 2006: 115). Here we can see an interesting change in the case form of the relevant pronoun, as follows:

(9) a. That poor *I* must write helter-skelter. (1832 Gaskell, *Letters* 2 p. 2; Fischer and van der Wurff (2006: 115))
   b. The miserable little *me* to be taken up and loved after tearing myself to pieces (1879 *Meredith, Egoist* xlviii 606; Fischer and van der Wurff (2006: 115))

The older subjective or nominative case[12] comes to be replaced by objective or accusative case. This is a ModE development. It is a part of the drift in English personal pronouns towards objective forms in subjective contexts. That is to say, objective case can be used instead of the expected subjective case in PDE, while subjective case was the only choice previously.

Although the prototypical heads of NPs are nouns and pronouns, other categories can serve that function, as follows (from Denison (1998: 114)):

(10) a. the *poor* (poor people)
    b. the *French* (French people)
    c. the *unknown* (that which is unknown)
    d. the *deceased* (the dead person, cf. dead people)

The above construction can be analyzed in two different ways. One is to assume that a head noun, like *people* (e.g. *the poor people*) or *thing* (e.g.

---

12) Barber (1976: 232) also gives several Early ModE examples (e.g. from Shakespeare):

  I Lady, you are the crull'st *shee* aliue. (*Twelfth Night*)
  ii. and to poore *we*
     Thine enmities most capitall (*Coriolanus*)
  iii. Who ere shee bee,
     That not impossible *shee*
     That shall command my heart and mee (Richard Crashaw)
  iv. and hee of *Wales*, that gaue Amamon the Bastinado (*Henry IV Part I*)

But objective case could be used in the same context:

  v. But to the highest *him*, that is behight
     Father if Gods and men by equal might; (Spenser, *Faerie Queene*)

the unknown thing) is missing by ellipsis. Another possible account is to assume that the adjective itself is the head in an NP. According to Rissanen (1999: 199), adjectives have been used as heads in an NP in early English. In OE and ME, the adjective head had a more extensive sphere of reference than today. It could refer, for instance, to a single person or a specific group of persons or things. This means that such an expression as *the poor* could mean "(a) specific poor person(s)" at the previous stage of English, as we see in (11), while it can only mean "the poor people in general" in PDE:

(11) *The younger* [sing.] rises when *the old* [sing.] doth fall.
(Shakespeare, *Timon of Athens* I. i; Rissanen (1999: 200))

"The singular, nongeneric types are hardly productive now, being largely confined to fixed expressions," like (10d) (Denison 1998: 114).

5.2.2. Determiners

As we have already seen in Section 4.3, OE had no articles, properly speaking. Where we would use a definite article, the Anglo-Saxons often used one of the demonstratives (such as *se* 'that' or *þes* 'this'); and, where we would use an indefinite article, they sometimes used either the numeral *ān* 'one' or *sum* 'a certain.'[13]

---

13) "When a language develops an article system ... it usually does so using a limited number of sources, e.g. definite articles from demonstrative pronouns, indefinite articles from the numeral 'one' or sometimes from a quantifier (e.g. *sum* in OE)."

In PDE the determiner slot can only be filled by one element. To put it other way, it is impossible to use more than one determiner in front of the same noun; *the this book, *my the book, *which your book, *some the book, etc. However, this was not the case in the earlier stage of English. For example, in OE "we find combinations of possessive and demonstrative pronouns, and also genitive phrases and demonstratives, as in *on Godes þa gehalgodan cyricean* 'in God's the hallowed church' (*HomU* 20 (*BlHom* 10) (66)), and *se heora ayrwyrð bisceop* 'the their venerable bishop' (*LS* 25(MichaelMor) 88)" (Fischer and van der Wurff 2006: 120). The following is the Early ModE and the Late ModE examples from Barber (1976: 234) and Denison (1998: 115), respectively:

(12) a. *this your* moste noble realme (Elyot, *Governor*)
    b. Forgiue me *this my* Vertue (Shakespeare, *Hamlet*)
    c. all *those his* Lands (Shakespeare, *Hamlet*)
    d. At *each his* needlesse heauings (Shakespare, *Winter's Tale*)
    e. of *euery These* happened accidents
       (Shakespare, *The Tempest*)
(13) a. They are great Men doubtless but how are they to be compared to *those our* countreymen Milton and the two Sidneys. (1818 Keats, *Letters* 94 p. 234 (Oct.))
    b. which have already been highly approved of in *this their* new form by my daughters (1864 Gaskell, *Letters* 545 p. 723 (1 Jan.))

In the Early ModE period the definite article was sometimes written *th*

(Fischer and van der Wurff 2006: 116)

or *th'* before vowels, representing a pronunciation [ð], as in *themperour* 'the emperor' (Elyot), *th'Oke* 'the Oke' (Milton). "In dramatic dialogue we also find forms like *ith* 'in the' and *ath* 'of the, on the', which can occur before consonants as well as vowels, as in *King Lear*'s *i'th'clout* 'in the target'" (Barber 1976: 225).

The negative determiner *no* had the alternative form *none* in the Early ModE period, so the distribution of the two forms was the same as for *a/an*. In other words, *no* was used before consonants and *none* before vowels (e.g. *no gentyl men* vs. *none ornament*).

Demonstratives are binary in PDE; proximal *this/these* vs distal *that/those*. But Early ModE had a trinary system; *this, that* and *yon*. *Yon* had variant forms like *yond* and *yonder*. In this system *this* implies 'near the speaker' and *that* implies 'remote from the speaker', while *yon(d(er))* implies 'remote from both the speaker and the hearer' and carries the additional implication 'visible, in sight' (Barber 1976: 228). This can be illustrated by a famous passage from the first scene of *Hamlet*:

(14) Last night of all,
　　　When *yond* same Starre that's Westward from the Pole
　　　Had made his[14] course t'illume *that* part of Heauen
　　　Where now it burnes, Marcellus and my selfe,
　　　The Bell then beating one -

Yon(d(er)) disappeared from English, probably because the referential meaning of *yon(d(er))* overlaps with that of *that*. 'Remote from both the

---

14) Here *his* is the possessive form of *it*, not of *he,* meaning 'its'.

speaker and the hearer' is a part of 'remote from the speaker'.

Next, let us consider pre- and post-determiners shortly. OE (15), ME (16) and Early ModE (17, from Barber (1976: 234)) had more pre-determiners that occur before the central determiner. That is, not a few PDE post-determiners could occur in front of the central determiner, acting as pre-determiners, as follows (Fischer 1992: 211):

(15) *ælc* an hagelstan 'each a hailstone'
   (*HomU* 36 (Nap 45) 51)
(16) *some* þe messangers 'some the angels'
   (*Glo. Chron.* A (Clg) 2718)
(17) a. In *eight* the first yeeres of his empire (Elyot, *Governor*)
   b. and behold *two* the most prodigious rascals that euer slipt into the shape of men (Middleton, *A Trick to Catch the Old One*)

This pattern is not possible any more. Instead we should say *each hailstone, some angels, the first eight years* and *the two most prodigious rascals*.

5.3. Internal Structure of the Verb Phrase

In a full sentence, there must be a predicate, along with a subject. The predicate composes a verb phrase (VP) categorically. The predicate can also contain noun phrases (e.g. as its object or complement),[15] adjective phrases

---

15) It is well-perceived that the term 'complement' is conceptually evasive. Its clear notion is difficult to define. The term is sometimes used in the sense of a 'predicative (complement)' (especially in school grammars). In the meantime, it also has the broader notion adopted in modern linguistics, where it is any element

(e.g. as its complement) and prepositional phrases (e.g. as its adverbial expression).16) But the kernel part of the predicate is the verbal group, which is the combination of a lexical main verb (obligatory) and all accompanying auxiliaries (optional). The verbal group functions as the predicator in a sentence17) and 16 different types are used in PDE, as follows:

Table 5.2 Internal Structure of the Verbal Group of Present-day English

(Modal)	(Perf=HAVE)	(Prog=BE)	(Pass=BE)	Lexical Verb	Type
				takes/took	1
may/might				take	2
	has/have/had			taken	3
		am/are/is was/were		taking	4
			is/am/are/ was/were	taken	5
may/might	have			taken	6
may/might		be		taking	7
may/might			be	taken	8
	has/have/had	been		taking	9
	has/have/had		been	taken	10
		am/are/is was/were	being	taken	11
may/might	have	been		taking	12
may/might	have		been	taken	13

licensed by a particular head. Under this notion, an object is just a type of a verbal complement. To know more about the notion of complement, see Lee (2008).
16) An adverbial expression is sometimes called an adjunct.
17) So we should say Subject-Predicator-Object (SPO), instead of Subject-Verb-Object (SVO), since a verb is a term for word classes, not for grammatical functions.

may/might		be	being	taken	14
	has/have/had	been	being	taken	15
may/might	have	been	being	taken	16

Dummy=DO	Lexical Verb
Do you ... / You *do* not ...	take

Here it should be noticed that each auxiliary verb determines the form of the verb that follows it and that there is a strict order between the verbs. The most extended form of the verbal group (Type 16) is the one like the following:

(18) By 1.30 I *must have been being introduced* in the dark, large hall of the place to Miss Heimann and Miss Jeaffreson, who had been getting their things on. (c1927 Ford Madox Ford, *The Marsden Case* ii.18)

However, the maximal number of the verbal group was three in OE, as follows:

Table 5.3 Internal Structure of the Verbal Group of Old English

(Modal)	(Perf=HAVE)	Lexical Verb
	(Prog=BE)	
	(Pass=BE)	

In other words, the sequences of Perfective-Progressive, Perfective-Passive, Progressive-Passive, and Perfective-Progressive-Passive were not possible in OE. Therefore, the following constructions have been introduced into

English since the OE times:

(19) a. Perfective-Progressive-Lexical Verb
   (e.g. *has/have/had been taking*) [Type 9]
   b. Perfective-Passive-Lexical Verb
   (e.g. *has/have/had been taken*) [Type 10]
   c. Progressive-Passive-Lexical Verb
   (e.g. *am/are/is being taken*) [Type 11]
   d. Modal-Perfective-Progressive-Lexical Verb
   (e.g. *may/might have been taking*) [Type 12]
   e. Modal-Perfective-Passive-Lexical Verb
   (e.g. *may/might have been taken*) [Type 13]
   f. Modal-Progressive-Passive-Lexical Verb
   (e.g. *may/might be being taken*) [Type 14]
   g. Perfective-Progressive-Passive-Lexical Verb
   (e.g. *has/have/had been being taken*) [Type 15]
   h. Modal-Perfective-Progressive-Passive-Lexical Verb
   (e.g. *may/might have been being taken*) [Type 16][18]

The dummy auxiliary *do* was not used in OE and ME, either. It was introduced into English after the 16th century.

From the types of the verbal group exemplified in (19), we can see that the first auxiliary or lexical verb (when there is no auxiliary) carries tense and is therefore finite. Other verbs are all nonfinite. Finite verb-forms occur either in the present or in the past. Nonfinite verb-forms come in four

---

18) However, the constructions with more than three auxiliary verbs are rare in English.

types: *to*-infinitive (e.g. *I want him to dance.*), bare infinitive (e.g. *I saw him dance.*), present participle (e.g. *He is dancing.*) and past participle (e.g. *He has often danced.*).

Our main concern of this section is to review the process and the period of the extension of the English verbal group.[19]

5.3.1. Tense

If we accept the argument that "'tense' is a grammatical term referring to specific verbal forms which has a relation with the notional ideas of 'time'" (Fischer and van der Wurff 2006: 131), English has only two tenses; past and present. An English verb has no inflectional form to express the future time, so English has no future tense. Instead, other methods are employed to express future time; the use of an independent auxiliary *will/shall*, the mere use of the simple present or the present progressive, etc. And perfective and progressive forms are regarded aspectual expressions rather than different tenses.

OE also had only two tenses and these were used more or less in the same way as in PDE. "The present tense was used to refer to the here and now, and also to timeless truths or situations (including habitual actions), while the past tense was employed to express any event that belonged to the past, including events for which we would now use a perfect or pluperfect (i.e. past perfect)" (Fischer and van der Wurff 2006: 131). OE did not have future tense, either. Instead, for example, the simple present

---

[19] For the more detailed discussion of the extension of the English verbal group, see Lee (1999a: Chapter 13; 1999b).

was used to express futurity, sometimes accompanied by a relevant adverbial expression, as in the following:

(20) Ic *arise* of deaðe on ðæm þriddan dæge
  = I *arise* from death on the third day
   'I *will arise* from the dead on the third day'
   (*ÆCHom* I, 10 (259.27); Fischer and van der Wurff (2006: 132))

The periphrastic future expression, which is formed with the help of auxiliaries such as *shall/will*, is a much later development.

Broadly saying, the tense system of English has not changed very much since the OE times.

5.3.2. Auxiliaries

As shown in Table 5.2, English auxiliaries are divided into five groups; modal auxiliaries, the perfective auxiliary *have*, the progressive auxiliary *be*, the passive auxiliary *be* and the dummy auxiliary *do*. The perfective auxiliary *have* and the progressive auxiliary *be* may be grouped together as aspectual auxiliaries.

In this section we will see what changes English auxiliaries have undergone during the last centuries.

5.3.2.1. Modal Auxiliaries

It is widely assumed that in OE and probably in ME too, modals were not auxiliaries but lexical verbs, as the following examples, where modals take object NPs or clauses, evidence:

(21) a. ... þat he geornor *wolde* sibbe wið hiene þonne gewinn
= ... that they rather *wanted* peace with him than conflict
'... that they wanted peace with him rather than conflict'
(*Orosius* 3 1 96.17)
b. ... Deme ge nu, swa swa ge *willion* þæt eow sy eft gedemed
= ... Judge you now, as you *wish* that to-you be afterward judged
'Judge now as you wish to be judged later'
(*HomS* 17(Bl 5) 130)
c. She *koude* muchel of wandryge by the weye
'She *knew* a lot about travelling.' (*CT* I. 467 [1: 469])

The examples given above also show that the ancestors of PDE modal auxiliaries, which are sometimes called pre-modals, had lexical meanings; *cunnan/cann* 'know how to, have the power to, be able', *magan/may* 'be strong, sufficient, in good health, be able to', *motan*[20]/*must* 'be allowed to, be obliged to' *sculan/shall* 'owe, be necessary' and *willan* 'will, wish, want, desire'. And pre-modals, like lexical full verbs, could take inflectional endings, as in *þu cannst* (> *thou canst*), *we cunnon* and *we cuðon*.

Pre-modals have developed into auxiliary-like element since the OE period by the loss of lexical meanings, by the loss of all direct object

---

20) Here an **asterisk** (*) means that the element is a reconstructed term, to be distinguished from historically attested terms. Linguistic reconstruction is the practice of establishing the features of the unattested ancestor (proto-language) of one or more given languages.

constructions, and by the loss of the inflectional paradigm.[21] This change was gradual. The change that English pre-modals underwent is a representative case of grammaticalization. Grammaticalization is a process whereby a lexical item, with full referential meaning (i.e. an open-class element), develops grammatical meaning (i.e. it becomes a closed-class element).[22] This process is often accompanied by a reduction in or loss of phonetic substance, loss of syntactic independence and of lexical (referential) meaning. The notable feature of grammaticalization is that it is gradual. For example, the loss of lexical meanings cannot be abrupt.

5.3.2.2. Aspectual Auxiliaries

Aspect is not easily distinguished from tense. Aspect is "a concept which refers to the way the meaning of the main verb is viewed in time" (Aarts 2001: 37). The main categories of aspect in English are the perfect and the progressive. They convey completed activity, and activity in progress or of limited duration, respectively. Nevertheless, they involve the system of tense, too, since the perfect is used for past events (usually with 'current relevance') and the progressive for future reference. According to Fischer and van der Wurff (2006: 135), "the differences between OE and PDE in the way the *be+ing* form and *have*+past participle were used are quite considerable."

---

21) So modal auxiliaries do not take the third person singular present-tense verbal ending -(e)s in PDE; *He cans do it*.

22) Another well-known case of **grammaticalization** is the development of English future auxiliary *be going to* from the progressive form of the lexical verb *go*.

5.3.2.2.1. Progressive Auxiliary

The OE progressive was the form of *beon/wesan* 'be' (sometimes *weorðan* 'become') plus the present participle in *-ende*.23) During the ME period the progressive ceased to be expressed by a verb *be* plus *-ende*, and was replaced by a verb *be* plus *-ing*. "There is considerable disagreement concerning the origin of the progressive *-ing*" (Traugott 1972: 143). The common view is that it has been derived from the OE gerund or verbal noun ending *-ung*, as in OE *leornung* 'learning' (that is, knowledge) and *bodung* 'preaching' (that is, sermon) from *leornian* 'to learn' and *bodian* 'to announce, preach' (Pyles and Algeo 1993: 163).24) At first, the progressive with a verbal noun ending occurred with the preposition *on* (22a) or *in* (especially in ME, (22b)). Later, *on/in* (sometimes *at*) were often reduced to [ə(n)], giving such forms as *an-* or *a-* (22c):25)

(22) a. in a perspectiue glasse hee set before his eyes king Henrie the eight with all his Lordes *on* hunting in his gorrest at Windsore. (Nashe *UT* II.253.23; Traugott (1972: 143))
   b. While this gode was *in* gederyng the grestts among, Antenor to the temple trayturly yode

---

23) On the different forms of the verb *be* in OE, refer to Section 4.6.
24) See Section 4.6, too.
25) Such adjectives as *abroad, afield, abed, asleep* are also from a prepositional expression like [*on board*] (> *a-board* > *aboard*). So it is naturally explained why these adjectives cannot be used as a pre-modifier for a noun (*news abroad*, cf. *abroad news), since a prepositional modifier cannot be used prenominally in English (e.g. *a plan for the new office*, cf. **a for the new office plan*).

> = While this wealth was *in gathering* the persons-of-rank among Antenor to the temple treacherously went
> 'While this wealth was being collected among the nobility, Antenor treacherously went to the temple.' (c1450(?a1400) *Destr.Troy* 11735; Denison (1993: 388))

c. Now might I doe it, but now a is <u>*a-praying*</u>,
And now Ile doo't, and so a goes to heaven.[26]
(Shakespeare *Hamlet* III. iii. 73-4)

Besides the formal changes of the progressive, their function was also differentiated. The progressive was used less frequently than today in early English (cf. Barber (1976: 261)).[27] The simple present was used where the progressive should be used in PDE, as in the following Early ModE example:

(23) Soft!, he *wakes*. 'Silent!, he *is waking*.'
(Shakespeare, *Richard III;* Barber (1993: 261))

The converse is also true. In PDE we can use the progressive form only for actions and happenings. So we do not say "I am knowing" or "They are liking". In OE, however, the progressive is often found with emotional and

---

[26] This example also shows that in the Early ModE period *he* could be weakened to *a* when it was not stressed. See Section 4.2.

[27] "Although OE could form verb phrases just as we do by combining the verbs for 'have' and 'be' with participles (as in Modern English *has run* and *is running*), it did so less frequently, and the system of such combinations was less fully developed." (Pyles and Algeo 1993: 130)

stative verbs, such as *wylnian* 'desire', *wunian* 'dwell', *libban* 'live', and others:

(24) a. Ða cwæð Tyberius: Eala, swyðe *wæs* ic *gewylnigende* þæt ic hyne geseon wolde.
   = Then said Tiberius, lo, strongly *was* I *desiring* (now *desired*) that I him see would
   'Then Tiberius said, "Lo, my desire to see him was very strong.'
   (*VSal* 1 (Cross)33.1; Fischer and van der Wurff (2006: 136))
   b. þæt seo ea *bið flowende* ofer eal Ægypta land
   = that this river *is flowing* (now *floods*) over all Egyptians' land
   (*Orosius* 12.35; Traugott (1972: 90))

We can see through the examples (23)-(24) that the use of the progressive was at first optional and freely interchangeable with the simple present. Generally, the progressive was used less frequently than today. The construction became obligatory for the action at the time of speaking and in contexts describing limited duration only in the Late ModE period.

The construction of using the progressive to express futurity, as in *We are leaving at six*, was not used in OE, either. It becomes common only in the Early ModE period but is first restricted to verbs of motion. Later, other activity verbs are found here too.[28]

---

28) We use the present progressive to express what we have already arranged to do in the future. So its use is not limited to the verbs of motion. It is widely used with dynamic verbs in general:

　i. I *am* not *working* tomorrow, so we can go somewhere.
　ii. Sam *isn't playing* football on Saturday. He hurt his leg. (Murphy 2001: 36)

5.3.2.2.2. Perfective Auxiliary

The past and the present perfect can both refer to past time but they express an activity differently. When we use the present perfect, there is 'a connection with now'. It is used to express 'the action having a result now (e.g. *I have forgotten his name.*)' and 'a recent happening (e.g. *I've just had lunch.*)', and 'a period of time continuing from the past until now (e.g. *Have you ever eaten a caviar?*)'. In the meantime, the past tense express 'a finished time'. However, the distinction between the two systems were not so clear at the previous stage of English. So they were mere variants for a while. They could be used interchangeably, although there may be differences in semantic and pragmatic nuances:[29]

(25) a. The Englishman ... *has murdered* (now *murdered*) young Halbert ... yesterday morning (Galsworthy, *In Chancery*; Fischer and van der Wurff (2006: 139))
   b. Beleeue me Lords, for flying the Brookes,
   I *saw* not (now *haven't seen*) better sport these seuen yeere day (Shakespeare, *Henry VI Part* 2; Barber (1976: 262))

Previously, the past tense form was used more widely. The perfect could be used more widely since the OE times and become more firmly fixed

---

[29] Even in PDE the two constructions are not mutually exclusive, as follows:

  i. I *have* just *had* lunch. vs. I just *had* lunch.
  ii. I've already *mailed* it. vs. I already *mailed* it.
  iii. I *haven't mailed* it yet. vs. I *did*n't *mail* it yet.

later.30)

One thing to note finally in relation to the perfect is that there was another perfective auxiliary, i.e. *be*, used in OE, ME and Early ModE, along with *have*. "In Germanic languages generally, including OE, the perfect of certain verbs was formed not with *have* but with *be*. These verbs were intransitive verbs, typically with meanings in the area of movement and change of state" (Denison 1993: 344), as follows (from Denison (1993: 359)):

(26) a. oþþæt wintra *bið* þusend *urnen* [OE]
   = until winters *is* thousand *run*
   'until a thousand years *have passed*' (*Phoen* 363)
   b. Whanne he *escaped was* [ME]
   'When he *has escaped*'
   (c1375 Chaucer, *CT.Mk.* VII 2735)
   c. yet Benedicke was such another; and now *is* he *become* a man [Early ModE] (1623 Shakespeare, *Ado* III. iv. 86)

However, the *be*-perfect disappeared from English, leaving some historical residues like *Spring is come* and *He was gone before I arrived*.31) The *be*-perfect construction could be confused with the passive, since they have the same structure, i.e. *be*+past participle. Ambiguity could arise here.32)

---

30) "The perfect marking is very common in our period (in the Early ModE period, author's addition), but perhaps not quite as common as it is today: occasionally, a writer uses a past tense where we should use a perfect." (Barber 1976: 262)
31) These remaining constructions can be analyzed into [*be*+adjective], not into [*be*+past participle].

Chapter 5 | Changes in Grammar: Syntactic Change   143

5.3.2.3. Passive Auxiliary

Originally, Germanic languages had passive inflectional endings, but the endings all disappeared at a prehistoric stage. The only remnant in OE is observed in the verb *hatan* 'call, name':

(27) and se munuc *hatte* abbo
   = and that monk *was-called* Abbo
   (*ÆLS* II 32.3; Denison (1993: 421))

These inflectional passive forms were eventually lost. Instead,[33] the periphrastic passive was formed in OE with the help of the auxiliaries like *beon/wesan* 'be' and *weorþan* 'become':[34]

---

32) "The combination of *be*+past participle was functionally at a disadvantage because it was ambiguous: it was also used for the passive construction. Thus a phrase like *she was returned* could mean 'she had returned' as well as 'she had been returned'. In addition, the common abbreviation of both *has* and *is* to *'s* led to a further falling-together of the *be* and *have* verbs, under the more frequent perfect auxiliary *have*." (Fischer and van der Wurff 2006: 142)

33) "Another OE alternative for the modern passive was the indefinite pronoun *man* 'one', as in *Hine man hēng* 'Him one hanged', that is, 'He was hanged.'" (Pyles and Algeo 1993: 130)

34) **Periphrasis** is a device by which a grammatical category or relationship is expressed by a free morpheme (typically one or more function words modifying a content word), instead of being shown by inflection or derivation. For example, the English future tense is periphrastic: it is formed with an auxiliary verb (*shall* or *will*) followed by the base form of the main verb. Another example is the comparative and superlative forms of adjectives when they are formed with the words *more* and *most* rather than with the suffixes *-er* and *-est*. So the forms *more beautiful* and *most*

(28) a. Þær _wæron_ gehælede þurh ða halgan femnan fela adlige menn[35]

 = There _were_ healed through the blessed woman many sick men

 'Many sick men were healed by the blessed woman'

 (_ÆLS_ I 20.113; Denison (1993: 418))

 b. and hi _wurdon_ ða utan _ymbsette_ mid Romaniscum here swa lange þæt ...

 = and they _were/became_ then from-outside _besieged_ with/by Roman army so long that ...

 'and they were then besieged by the Roman army for so long that ...' (_ÆCHom_ I 28.402.33; Denison (1993: 419))

At first, the _weorþan_ construction was probably used to denote process rather than state. Later, however, the difference in meaning between _beon/wesan_ 'be' and _weorþan_ 'become' became indistinct. Then a tendency arose to use the _beon/wesan_ form only.

After the loss of the _weorþan_ construction, a new way was introduced to express the difference between process and result. It is to use _get_ as a new passive auxiliary:[36]

(29) A certain Spanish pretending Alchymist ... _got acquainted_ with foure

---

 beautiful are periphrastic (or analytic), while _lovelier_ and _loveliest_ are inflectional (or synthetic). The English passive is periphrastic, too.

[35] At first, the agent was introduced by the preposition _fram_ 'from' or _þurh_ 'through' rather than _by_.

[36] The passive _get_ is used to say that something happens to somebody or something, especially if this is unplanned or unexpected. We use _get_ only when things happen or change. cf. Murphy (2001: 82)

rich Spanish merchants

(1652 Gaule, *Magastrom.* 361 (*OED* s.v. *get* v. 34b); Denison (1993: 419))

The first instances of a new process passive with *get* are encountered in the 17th century and have become very popular since then (cf. Fischer and van der Wurff (2006: 153), Denison (1993: 419)).

5.3.2.4. Dummy Auxiliary *Do*

One of the English-particular grammatical features is the obligatory use of *do* in negative and interrogative sentences when there is no other auxiliary present. In these cases *do* is used as an empty 'operator'. That is, it is a purely grammatical element without any referential meaning.

Before the introduction of the dummy *do*, the main verb itself moves to the front in interrogative sentences, and in negative sentences the negative particle *ne* (OE) or *nat/not* (ME and ModE) was positioned (before in OE or)[37] after the main verb. Some Early ModE examples may be given:

(30) a. *Looks* it not like the king? (Shakespeare, *Hamlet* I. i. 43)
　　b. How *cam'st* thou hither? (Barber 1976: 263)
　　c. Why *lookes* your Grace so heauily today?
　　　(Barber 1976: 263)

---

37) The OE negative particle *ne* came before (rather than after) the main verb it modified: Ic *ne* dyde 'I not did', meaning 'I didn't do'. For the development of English negative expressions, refer to section 5.3.3.

(31) a. I *saw not* better sport these seuen yeeres day. (=(25b))

   (Shakespeare, *Henry VI Part* 2; Barber (1976: 262))

   b. It *serveth not* 'It doesn't serve. (it's no use.)'

   (c1513 Aoun, *The Battle of Flodden* I. 46)

   c. What it means I *know not*

   (1769 Woorforde, *Diary* I 95.8 (17 Dec.))

   d. I *doubt not* of her happiness in a future Life[38]

   (1785 Woorforde, *Diary* II 171.18 (23 Jan.))

The development of the dummy auxiliary *do* is one of the most interesting developments in the history of auxiliaries in English. It will not be discussed here how *do*-support[39] came to be introduced into English.[40] Whatever the sources of the dummy *do* are, it has been used extensively in all types of writing in the Early ModE period. Today, the insertion or omission of the auxiliary *do* is strictly regulated, whereas in Early ModE its use was optional, and it could be inserted or omitted at will. In other words, the Early ModE *do*-support was more liberal than in PDE. It was not required in interrogative and negative sentences, as in (30)-(31), and was allowed in affirmative declarative sentences without any meaning emphasis, as follows:

(32) a. Thus conscience *does* make cowards of us all

   (Shakespeare, *Hamlet* II. i. 83)

---

[38] For a long time after the introduction of *do*, some verbs resisted the use of *do* in negative sentences. They include *care, come, doubt, know, mistake* and *speak*. (cf. Barber (1976: 267))

[39] The process of inserting *do* is called *do*-support in the linguistic literature.

[40] For this topic, see Lee (1993) and the references cited there.

b. Upon my secure hour thy uncle stole,
   With juice of cursed hebenon in a vial,
   And in the porches of my ears *did* pour
   The leperous distilment. (Shakespeare, *Hamlet* I. v. 6l)

In the course of the Early ModE period, however, the use of the auxiliary *do* gradually became regulated. It became increasingly normal to insert *do* in interrogative and negative sentences and to omit it from affirmative declarative ones (except when emphasis was required). According to Barber (1976: 265), the regulating process began in the middle of the 16th century and was very nearly completed by 1700. Now it is a strict rule to follow.

5.3.2.5. Combination of Auxiliaries

We have said in the introduction of this section that the sequences of Perfective-Progressive, Perfective-Passive, Progressive-Passive, and Perfective-Progressive-Passive were not used in OE at all. A large number of new periphrastic constructions, as exemplified in (19), have developed since the ME period to express tense, mood and aspect distinctions more minutely.

In OE, for example, the perfective *have* could be found with (a past participle of) a lexical verb only, as we can see in Table 5.3. But it came to occur in combinations with the passive *be* (i.e. Perfective-Passive, the first attested example is (33a)) and the progressive *be* in ME (i.e. Perfective-Progressive, the first attested example is (34a)).

(33) a. He ... haffde himm sellf wel filled / All þatt tatt *cwiddedd haffde ben* / Off himm ...

'He had himself quite fulfilled everything that *had been said* about him'

(c1180 *Orm* 19308 (cited from *OED Well, adv.* 12)

b. We *habbeoð i-beon* an hirede; hæhliche *iwurðed*, þurh þinne stiwærd; ...

'We *have been* in court highly *honoured* by your steward'

(a1225 (?a1200) Lay.*Brut* (Clg)(EETS OS250, 277) 6772-3)

(34) a. þof he thre dais *had fastand bene*, O mete and frinc, ...

'though he *had been fasting* from food and drink for three days'

(a1400 (a1325) *Cursor* (Vsp)(EETS OS 57, etc.) 5256)

b. We *haue been watynge* al this fourenyght ...

(c1386 Chaucer, *CT Kn.* A 929)

The combination of Progressive and Passive, which results in the double *be*, i.e. *be-being*, was much later than the introduction of the Perfective-Progressive and the Perfective-Passive patterns, since the first reliable example, (35a), is from the year of 1772:

(35) a. I have received the speech and address of the House of Lords; probably, that of the House of Commons *was being debated* when the post went out.

(1772 *A Series of Letters of the First Earl of Malmesbury* (ed. the Earl of Malmesbury, London 1870) I.264, letter from Mr Harris, Jun., to his mother, 8.xii.1772)

b. The inhabitants of Plymouth are under arms, and everything *is*

Chapter 5 | Changes in Grammar: Syntactic Change   149

being done that can be.

(1779 *A Series of Letters of the First Earl of Malmesbury* (ed. the Earl of Malmesbury, London 1870) I.430, letter from Mrs Harris, Jun., to her son, 22.viii.1779)

c. while my hand *was being Drest* by a Mr. Young, I spoke for the first time ...

(1797 Coleridge, *Collected Letters* (ed. E. L. Griggs, Oxford 1956) I.312, letter of March 1797 to Thos. Poole.)

Before the progressive passive developed, the simple progressive[41] or the simple passive was used to deliver a passive sense, as in the following:

(36) a. Coming home tonight, a drunken boy *was carrying* ('was being carried') by our Constable to our new pair of stocks ...
(1663 *The Diary of Samuel Pepys* (ed. R. Latham and W. Matthews, London 1971) vol 4, April 12.)
b. and while Supper *is making* ('is being made') ready ...
(1684 Bunyan, *Pilgrim's Progress* 259.22)
(37) he found that the coach had sunk greatly on one side, though it *was* still *dragged* ('was still being dragged') by the horses;
(1838-9 Dickens, *Nickleby* v.52)

In conclusion, English has generalized possibilities of combination within the verbal group. By generalizing the combinatory possibilities of the auxiliaries, English could get strong devices to express delicate aspectual nuances.

---

41) The construction like (36) is called "passival", "covert passive", "passival active" or "passival progressive".

5.3.3. Negation

Negation is normally expressed by a negative adverb. In PDE this is typically *not*. Meanwhile, OE used the adverb *ne* 'not' and it came before the verb it modified.[42] Consequently, it contracted with (technically saying, procliticized to) the following verb, as in *nis* (*ne is* 'is not'), *nille* (*ne wille* 'will not') and *næfð* (*ne hæfð* 'has not'):

(38) a. ac we him *ne cunnon* æfterspyrigean
= but we them *not* know-how-to after-follow
'but we do not know how to follow in their footsteps'
(*CP* 5.16)
b. *Nolde* se Hælend for his bene swaþeah hym fram gewitan
= *not*-wanted the Lord for his prayer however him from depart
'However, the Lord did not want to depart from him because of his prayer.' (*ÆHP* XIV.199)

Today we are prohibited from using more than one negative element in a single sentence, but multiple negation was widely used in earlier English, usually for emphasis:

(39) a. þæt heora *nan ne* meahte *nanes* wæpnes gewealdan[43] [OE]
= that of-them *none not* was able *no* weapon wield

---

42) Lee (2007: Chapters 1-3) gives a detailed discussion of the development of English negative expressions.
43) *Ne* can be attached to some indefinite quantifiers and adverbs, as well as to certain verbs; *ne+æfre* 'ever' → *næfre* 'never', *ne+ænig* 'any' → *nænig* 'none', *ne+an* 'one' → *nan* 'none', *ne+a* 'ever' → *na* 'never', and others.

'that no one of them was able to wield a weapon'
(*Orosius* 194.18)

b. þurh unweotennesse *ne* mei ha *nawt* sunegin [ME]
= through ignorance *not* can she *not* sin
(*Sawles Warde* 255.33)

c. I haue one heart, one bosome, and one truth,
And that *no* woman has, *nor neuer none*
Shall mistris be of it, saue I alone [ModE]
(Shakespeare, *Twelfth Night*; Barber (1976: 283))

During the ME period, *not*,[44] in succession to OE *ne*, became the dominant negative adverb in English:

(40) a. & spacc he *nohht* wiþþ tunge
= and spoke he *not* with tongue
'and he did not speak out loud' (c1180 *Orm.* 224)
b. for it sufficeþ *not* to be vnbounden, but if ...
= for it suffices *not* to be unbound unless ...
'for it is not enough to be unbound, unless ...'
(?c1425(?c1400) *Loll.Serm.* 1.243)

The difference between *ne* and *not* is that the latter is positioned after the verb it modifies. Before the introduction of the dummy auxiliary *do*, *not* was positioned after the main verb, as we can see in (31). Just as OE *ne* could contract with (i.e. procliticize to) the following verb, *not* could be

---

44) *Not* was from OE *ne-a-wiht* 'not-ever-anything': *ne-a-wiht* > *nawiht, nowiht* > *nauht, nawht* > *noht, noȝt, nout* > *not, nat*.

attached to the proceeding verb (e.g. *isn't, hasn't, can't*). In ModE, such contracted forms as *wilnot, shallnot, didnot, nylnot, nynnot, ninnat* were used. Now *cannot* is the only form to be used. Probably, contraction became possible when the meaning of negation was weakened.

5.4. Grammatical Functions

It is widely accepted that sentences are analyzed into subparts which are referred to as constituents. These constituents function differently in a sentence, so several different terms are used to indicate different functions: subject, predicate, (direct and indirect) object, complement and adjunct. Throughout its history, English has a stable system of grammatical functions in active sentences. Nevertheless, we can see some changes in the use of subjects and objects.

5.4.1. Subjects

As far as subjects are concerned, principal changes have to do with dummy subjects and empty subjects. In PDE nominative subjects are generally obligatory. But some exceptional cases are found, especially in informal speech, as follows (Fischer and van der Wurff 2006: 161):

(41) a. ø seems he is not coming back
   b. Unfortunately, however, when ø came to pour out tea ø realized did not have any milk or sugar (Helen Fielding, "Bridget Jones's Diary", *Daily Telegraph*, 2/5/1998, p. 24)

In (41a) dummy subject *it* is seen as null, while in (41b) *I* was deleted, since the subject is normally *I* in a diary. So there are two different types of subject deletion: deletion of dummy subjects and that of personal pronouns. Personal pronouns can be deleted when they are recoverable through the clues given in a context.

Null dummy subjects are plentifully attested in OE texts, too, as in (42a), although an overt dummy subject, i.e. *it/hit* was also possible, as in (42b):

(42) a. ø nis me earfoðe to geþoianne þeodnes willan
   = ø not is for-me difficult to endure the lord's will
      '(it) is not difficult for me to endure the lord's will'
      (*Guthlac* A, B 1065)
   b. *hit* is unieðe to gesecgenne hu monige gewin wæron
   = *it* is hard to say how many fights were
      'it is not hard to say how many fights there were'
      (*Orosius* I 12.52.8)

In ME texts, too, both null and overt dummy subjects are used side by side. After 1500, however, only the variant with overt dummy *it* survives in the written record. The overt nominative subject became obligatory in an English sentence.

In early English the deletion of a personal pronoun subject was possible if it was implied by the context, especially when the verb followed a clause that expressed the subject:

(43) a. ... ø wolde on ðam westene wæstmes tilian

= ... ø wanted in the wasteland crop grow

'... (he) wanted to grow a crop in the wasteland.'

(*ÆCHom* II, 10.86.176; Fischer and van der Wurff (2006: 162))

b. Hē þē æt sunde oferflāt, ø hæfde māre mægen

'He outstripped you at swimming, (he) had more strength.'

(Pyles and Algeo 1993: 131)

The phenomenon that a pronominal subject remains unexpressed, as in the above, is often termed *pro*-drop. *Pro*-drop is observed in modern languages like Italian, too.[45] In Italian the verb inflection is rich. The richness of inflection allows one to identify the person and number combination. OE also had a richer (verbal) inflectional paradigm than PDE, and this will be the major reason why *pro*-drop was permitted more freely. This argument may be supported by the fact that, until Early ModE, it was possible to omit a personal pronoun subject *thou*, since the verbal ending for *thou*, i.e. -(*e*)*st*, is so clear to conjecture the deleted subject:

(44) a. Hast thou neuer an eie in thy heade? *Can<u>st</u>* ø not heare, and twere not as good deede as drinke to break the pate on thee, I am a

---

45) See the following Italian examples (Haegeman 1991: 413):

I. Giacomo ha parlato.
=Giacomo has spoken.
ii. ø Ha parlato.
=ø Has spoken.
iii. Giacomo ha detto che ø ha parlato.
= Giacomo has said that ø has spoken.

Chapter 5 | Changes in Grammar: Syntactic Change   155

very villaine, come and be hanged, *hast* ø no faith in thee?
(Shakespeare *Henry IV Part I*; Barber (1976: 284))

b. Ha! what *art* ø, who thus maliciously hast awakned me?
(Congreve *Old Bachelor*; Barber (1976: 285))

"In PDE we can omit the second subject when two clauses are coordinated, but only if the two subjects are identical. In Early ModE, the second subject is sometimes omitted even though it is different from the first, provided there is some word in the first clause from which it can be extracted" (Barber (1976: 285). In the following example, the omission of *he* is possible in co-reference to *him* in the preceding clause, which type of deletion is impossible in PDE:

(45) Nor do we finde *him* forward to be sounded,
But with a crafty Madness ø *keepes* aloofe
(Shakespeare, *Hamlet*, Barber (1976: 285))

Anyway, the *pro*-drop possibility in English has been restricted to the degree that the nominative subject is obligatory in nearly all types of sentences.

On the other hand, the subject of an OE verb might be expressed twice: once as a pronoun at its appropriate place in the structure of the sentence and once as a phrase or clause in anticipation (Pyles and Algeo 1993: 131):

(46) And [þā þe þǣr tō lāfe wǣron], *hī* cōmon tō þæs carcernes dura
'And [those that were there as survivors], *they* came to that prison's door.'

This construction occurs in PDE, too, but is often considered inelegant. It was more frequent in OE.

5.4.2. Demise of Impersonal Constructions

In OE there was a group of verbs expressing various kinds of sensation and emotion, i.e. verbs with meanings like 'be ashamed', 'regret', 'be hungry', 'like', 'detest,' etc. The feature of these verbs is that they could be used without a subject:[46]

(47) *him* (dat.) ofhreow *ðæs mannes* (gen.)[47]
   = *to-him* pitied *because-of-the man*
   'He felt pity for the man.'
   (*ÆCHom* I 8.192.16)

In the impersonal construction an Experiencer is normally marked as dative or accusative, and a Source as genitive.[48] However, the Experiencer or the Source NP may appear as nominative, too:

(48) a. *se mæsse-preost* (nom.) *ðæs mannes* (gen.) ofhreow
   = *the priest* because-of-the man felt-pity
   'The priest felt pity for the man.'
   (*ÆLS* II 26.262)

---

46) For OE impersonal verbs, refer to Lee (1999a: Chapter 8).
47) Note here that in the impersonal construction the finite verb is 3 SG, agreeing with *pro*-subject.
48) An **Experiencer** is one who perceives something, and a **Source** is the place from which an action or emotion originates.

b. Ða ofhreow *ðam munece* (dat.) *ðæs hreoflian mægenleast* (nom.)
= then pitied to-the monk *the leper's feebleness*
'Then the monk felt pity for the leper's feebleness.'
(*ÆCHom* I 23.336.10)

From the Early ModE period, however, the patterns of (47) are not found any more.[49] The empty subject option was lost from English altogether and individual verbs had mostly become restricted to the pattern of either (48a) or (48b), since the nominative subject became obligatory.

5.4.3. Objects

Objects also have undergone a number of changes in their nature and marking. In PDE all objects are marked as objective, while OE objects could be marked in three different case forms (accusative, dative and genitive).[50] The following examples show that the same verb, e.g. *onfon* 'receive' and *folgian* 'follow, pursue', could take objects of different case forms:

---

49) Some Early ModE examples are given below:

   i. *Me nede* ('I need') not long for to beseche Her that hath power me to commaund
      (Wyatt, *Poems*; Barber (1976: 285))
   ii. *Me thought* ('I think' or 'It seems to me') that Glouster stumbled.
      (Shakespeare *Richard III*; Barber (1976: 285))
50) On the changes of the case forms of (pro)nominal elements, see Lee (1999a: Chapter 3).

(49) a. ... onfon *minne gast* (acc.)

　　'... receive my soul' (*ÆCHom* I, 29.426.14)

　b. Ac ge onfoþ *þæm mægene* (dat.) Halges Gastes

　= But you receive that power of-Holy Ghost

　　'But you receive the power of the Holy Ghost' (*Bl* 11)

　c. ... *deaðes* (gen.) onfoð

　= ... (he) ... death receives

　　'... he ... suffers death' (*ÆCHom* I, 21.308.2)

(50) a. ond ða folgode *feorhgeniðlan* (acc.)

　= and then pursed *deadly-foes*

　　'and then (he) pursued deadly foes' (*Beowulf* 2928)

　b. *Him* (dat.) folgiað fuglas scyne

　= *him* follow birds brilliant

　　'brilliant birds follow him' (*Phoen* 591)

It is argued that different case forms signify semantic differences. The accusative marking means complete and direct affectedness, the dative is a kind of incomplete or indirect affectedness, and the genitive shows some sort of partitive meaning.[51] The meaning differences are sensed in the examples given above. After the OE period, however, the formal distinction between accusative and dative disappeared from English because of the

---

51) "It is often noted that the NP expressing the source of an emotion or mental state such as caring, neglecting or enjoying is typically in the genitive; the NP expressing the affected or interested person (the **Experiencer** in the terminology used here, the author's addition) is typically dative with a verb of harming, (dis)pleasing, (dis)believing; and verbs of accusing, asking and depriving typically take the accusative of the person and the genitive of the thing." (Fischer and van der Wurff 2006: 164)

general levelling of inflectional endings. And the genitive object also disappeared completely. Now all objects have the same case form, i.e. accusative or objective.

5.4.4. Emergence of New Passives: Indirect Passive and Prepositional Passive[52]

For the verbs like *give*, PDE tends to allow two different kinds of complementation:

(51) a. Tom *gave* presents to Mary.
    b. Tom *gave* Mary presents.

There are corresponding passives for both patterns:

(52) a. Presents were *given* to Mary (by Tom).
    b. Mary was *given* presents (by Tom).[53]

We may call (52a) a direct passive; it is the conventional sort of passive whose subject corresponds to the direct object in the active. The type (52b) is often known as an indirect passive, since it takes as its subject an NP corresponding to the indirect object in the active.

---

52) For the detailed discussion of the appearance of the indirect passive and the prepositional passive, see Lee (1993; 1999a: Chapters 8 and 10; 2007).
53) Grammarians, e.g. Quirk *et al.* (1985: 327), claim that nowadays the indirect passive, like (52b), is the preferred form.

In OE the equivalent of (52a) was normal. But the indirect passive is an innovative construction. It was not present in OE and ME and began to occur from the late 14th century onwards.

Meanwhile, OE had a passive where the Benefactive, i.e. indirect object, remained in the dative case, as in the following:

(53) a. ac *him* (dat.) næs getiðod *ðære lytlan lisse* (gen.)
 = but *him* not-was granted *that small favour*
 'But *he* was not granted that small favour'
 (*ÆCHom* I 23.330.29)
 b. Sægde ðæt *hiere* (dat.) *niowan blod* (acc.) læten wære in earme
 = said that *her newly blood* let was in arm
 '(She) said that *she* had lately been bled blood from the arm'
 (*Bede* 5 3.392.2)

The pattern (53) is sometimes called an impersonal passive, since it lacks a nominative subject.

The reason why the indirect passive was not used in OE is that the subject of the OE passive construction would have been accusative in the active. That is, the nominative subject in the passive would have been an accusative object if not passivized:

(54) a. þæt he ongann to writenne *þa halgan Cristes boc* (acc.) ...
 'that he began to write *the book of holy gospel* ...'
 (*AHP* 1.25)

> b. ... swa swa *hit* (nom.) awriten is
>
> = as *it* written is
>
> 'as it is written' (*AHP* 15.107)

For this reason, the indirect object, marked dative, cannot be the nominative subject in the passive. The dative object should remain dative even in the passive. This is the impersonal passive.

ME onwards, however, the impersonal passive disappeared. Instead, the indirect passive was introduced. The first reasonably clear examples of the indirect passive are from the late 14th century, but they remained rare until late in the 15th century:

> (55) a. Item as for the Parke *she* is a lowyd Every yere a dere and xx Coupull of Conyes and all fewell Wode to her necessarye To be Takyn in a Wode callidde Grenedene Wode.
>
> 'Item: as for the park, *she* is allowed a deer each year and twenty pair of rabbits and all fuel wood necessary for her, to be taken in a wood called Greendene Wood'
>
> (1375 *Award Blount in ORS* 7 205.30)
>
> b. and *þey* shall be assigned redy shippyng and passage
>
> = and *they* shall be allotted ready shipping and passage
>
> (1418 *Let.War France in Bk Lond.E.* III.xvi 77.8)

Some later examples can be given:

> (56) a. where *we* were showed the place where the States-generall sit in council. (1660 *Pepys, Diary* I 140.2 (15 May))

b. *We* were allowed two hours for dinner.

(1817 Mary Shelley, *Six Weeks' Tour* 110.11)

The rise of the indirect passive is ascribed to the effacement of morphological distinction between accusative-dative contrast, which would have the effect of making the indirect object of an active sentence formally indistinguishable from the direct object. Both would have the same objective case. And the impersonal passive disappeared, since the nominative subject became obligatory in English after the OE times.

Another new passive construction that emerged after the OE period is the prepositional passive (P-passive, henceforth). P-passive is the construction where the object of a preposition in the active becomes the subject of the passive. P-passive, which is not found in OE, emerged in the ME period. The followings are the earliest examples, dated c. 1400 or earlier:[54]

(57) a. *heo* schal beo greattre ibolle, leafdiluker *leoten of* þen a leafdi of hames
  = *she* shall be greater honourd, lady-liker *thought of* than a lady of homes
  'she shall be more greatly honoured, thought of as more ladylike than a housewife' (*AW* 58.7)
 b. þer wes sorhe te seon hire leoflich lich *faren* so reowliche *wið*
  = there was sorrow to see her dear body *dealt* so cruelly *with*
  (c1225 *St Juliana* (Roy) 22.195)

---

55) The examples are mainly cited from Denison (1993). Refer to Denison (1993: 125-27) for more examples.

P-passive increases from the middle of the 14th century and came to be completely rooted into English at the end of the 15th century.

The standard and most widely accepted analysis for the possibility of P-passive is the reanalysis of [$_{VP}$ V [$_{PP}$ P NP]] into [$_{VP}$ [$_V$ V+P] NP], where P forms a new constituent with the preceding V, being lexicalized or forming a collocation such as *laugh at*. The concept of reanalysis should be harnessed to the word order change to provide an explanation for the sudden appearance of P-passive in ME (more exactly, in the 13th century). That is, the word order change during the ME period contributed to the unification of P into V, since the change from OE [$_{VP}$ [$_{PP}$ P NP] V] to ME [$_{VP}$ V [$_{PP}$ P NP]] made it possible to place V and P adjacently (> [$_{VP}$ [$_V$ V+P] NP]]. So the possibility of permitting P-passive is directly and entirely ascribed to the possibility of forming a [V+P] collocation.

There are a good many other syntactic differences that could be mentioned in this chapter. If all of them were mentioned here, the resulting list would suggest that early English, i.e. OE, ME and ModE, was far different from PDE in the grammatical structure. But the suggestion would be misleading, for the early and present stages of English are much more united by their similarities than divided by their differences. OE was also English and PDE has its root on OE.

Chapter 06

Changes in Meaning: Semantic Change

Like spellings, pronunciations, vocabulary, grammar and other aspect of language, the meanings of words (or morphemes) also change in various ways over time.[1] Thus "changes in the meanings of words - semantic change - can be among the most striking and accessible examples of language change. As words become used in different ways and in different contexts, it may acquire different associations, and so the meaning changes" (Culpeper 1997: 36).

6.1. Aspects of Meaning

The meaning of a word has several different aspects. It is more than the collection of definitions of a word we see in dictionaries. Knowing the meaning of a word is knowing how it is used.

---

1) For the more detailed treatment of the semantic changes in English, refer to Pyles and Algeo (1993: Chapter 10), Trask (1994: Chapter 8), Culpeper (1997: Chapter 6) and Campbell (2001: 254-73), among others.

It is necessary to distinguish between two aspects of meaning; the sense and the associations. The main meaning of a word is its sense, denotative meaning or literal meaning. But there is the equally important associative or connotative meaning.2) The connotative meaning is related to the language usage in actual discourse situations. Let us take an example. The words *woman* and *lady* have the nearly same denotative meaning (human, female and adult). But there must be more to meaning than this, since we know that there is a difference between these two words. For example, the following two sentences cannot be said to deliver the same meaning. They have different associations or connotations:

*Jane is only thirteen, but she's a woman already.*3)
*Jane is only thirteen, but she's a lady already.*4) (Culpeper 1997: 36-37)

---

2) **Denotation** is the literal meaning of a word, and **connotation** is the suggestive meaning of a word. For example, the word *city* connotes the attributes of largeness, populousness. It denotes individual objects such as London, New York, Paris. ("Connotation and Denotation" In *Wikipedia*. Retrieved July 31, 2018)

3) *Woman*: 1. An adult female human. 2. Women considered as a group; womankind: *"Woman feels the invidious distinctions of sex exactly as the black man does those of color"* (Elizabeth Cady Stanton). 3. An adult female human belonging to a specified occupation, group, nationality, or other category. ... (*The American Heritage Dictionary*, 4th edition, 2000)

4) *Lady* has more positive connotations than *woman*, as we can see through its meanings.

> *Lady*: 1. A well-mannered and considerate woman with high standards of proper behavior. 2a. A woman regarded as proper and virtuous. b. A well-behaved young girl. 3. A woman who is the head of a household. 4. A woman, especially when spoken of or to in a polite way. 5a. A woman to whom a man is romantically attached. b. *Informal* A wife. ... (*The American Heritage Dictionary*,

Sometimes the denotative or literal meaning changes, but the connotative or associative meaning can change, too. That is, words change in both their senses and associations. The change of association can often lead to the change of denotation. For instance, the (denotative) meaning of the word *sinister* was 'left' or 'left-handed', but this word had associations of bad luck, probably because using the left hand was not regarded as desirable in old times. Now this association formed the denotative meaning and its original denotative meaning, the notion of 'leftness' has died out.[5] So we should pay attention to both types of meaning together in considering meaning changes.

Many types of meaning change are found. It will be discussed below how and in what ways meaning changes.

6.2. Metaphoric and Metonymic Transfer of Meaning

There are a good many special types of transfer of meaning. The meaning transfer is involved with metaphoric or metonymic operations in many cases.[6] "Metaphor (from Greek *metaphorā* 'transference') involves

---

4th edition, 2000)

[5] *Sinister*: 1. Suggesting or threatening evil: *a sinister smile*. 2. Presaging trouble; ominous: *sinister storm clouds*. 3. Attended by or causing disaster or inauspicious circumstances. 4. On the left side; left. (*The American Heritage Dictionary*, 4th edition, 2000)

[6] A **metaphor** is an expression that ordinarily designates one concept (its literal meaning) but is used to designate another concept, thus creating an implicit comparison (Fromkin, Rodman and Hymes 2003: 204). There are so many examples including the following:

understanding or experiencing one kind of thing in terms of another kind of thing thought somehow to be similar in some way" (Campbell 2001: 258). For example, a lowest body part *foot* can mean the lowest part of all sorts of things, as in *foot of a mountain*, *foot of a bed* and *foot of a tree*.[7] We also use the word *leaf* to refer to a page in a book. This is the metaphoric transfer.[8]

In the meantime, "metonymy (from Greek *metōnomia* 'transformation of a name') is a shift in meaning from one thing to something connected with that thing, though it doesn't actually resemble it" (Denning and Leben 1995: 100). For instance, when we talk of the *throne* or the *crown*, meaning the person who sits on it (i.e. a king or queen), we use a metonymic shift. When a language is referred to as a *tongue*, when a soldier who wears a red coat is referred to as a *Redcoat*, and when *bread* means something to

---

i. Their new car turned out to be *a lemon*. (*Informal* "One that is unsatisfactory or defective") (cf. *lemon law* "a law obligating manufacturers or sellers to repair, replace, or refund the price of motor vehicles that prove to be defective")

ii. She is *a peach*. (*Informal* "a particularly admirable or pleasing person or thing")

When a metaphor is used frequently, it becomes conventional and we gradually stop perceiving it as a metaphor. For instance, 'Time is *money*' is such a 'dead' metaphor.

7) *Foot*: 1. The lower extremity of the vertebrate leg that is in direct contact with the ground in standing or walking. ... 3. Something suggestive of a foot in position or function, especially: a. The lowest part; the bottom: *the foot of a mountain*; *the foot of a page*. b. The end opposite the head, top, or front: *the foot of a bed*; *the foot of a parade*. ... (*The American Heritage Dictionary*, 4th edition, 2000)

8) The transfer of meaning is quite similar to the generalization of meaning, in that both types are all involved with the expansion of meaning. However, the meaning transfer is the expansion of meaning into a new category or a new field, unlike generalization.

eat in general, they are all examples of metonymy. If the word *foot* is used as a unit of measure, by adding to its original sense something like 'approximate length of the human foot,' this will be metonymic transfer, too. The use of the place for a product characteristic of it, as in *champagne* and *cognac*, from the name of the regions in France, *Champagne* and *Cognac*, is another case of metonymy.

There is a special kind of metonymy, called synecdoche, which "involves a part-to-whole relationship, where a term with more comprehensive meaning is used to refer to a less comprehensive meaning or vice versa: that is, a part (or quality) is used to refer to the whole, or the whole is used also to refer to part" (Campbell 2001: 260). *Hand* 'hired hand, employed workers', *sun* 'day', *moon* 'month' are such examples.

6.3. Synesthesia

Meaning may be transferred from one sensory faculty to another.[9] For example, such word as *clear*, originally describing sight, is used with reference to hearing, as in *clear-sounding*. This special type of meaning transfer is called synesthesia. There are more examples like this:

---

9) It is traditionally assumed that humans have at least five senses; sight, hearing, touch, smell, taste.

Table 6.1 Synesthesia

Words	Original Meaning Field	Transferred Meaning Field
loud	hearing	sight (*loud* colors)
sweet	taste	hearing (*sweet* music) or other senses (a *sweet* person)
smooth	touch	hearing (*smooth* music) or other senses (a *smooth* person)
warm	touch	sight (*warm* colors) and other senses (a *warm* person, a *warm* welcome)

6.4. Abstraction of Meaning

Concrete meanings may have abstract meanings. This is the abstraction of meaning.[10] The words like *understand* or *grasp* are examples of abstraction of meaning (in particular, from physical to mental), since their original meanings were 'to stand below/under or among'[11] and 'to hold something in your hand(s) firmly', respectively. The latter meaning is still used for *grasp*.[12] Likewise, the words like *comprehend* and *apprehend*[13] are also extended metaphorically to express the 'seizing' of something intellectually.

---

10) "It is frequently claimed that semantic shifts typically go from more *concrete* to more *abstract*. For example, there are many semantic changes which extend body part notions to more abstract meanings, but not the other way around." (Campbell 2001: 272)

11) ME *understanden*, from OE *understandan*: *under-* 'under-' + *standan* 'stand'.

12) *Grasp*: 1. To take hold of or seize firmly with or as if with the hand. 2. To clasp firmly with or as if with the hand. 3. To take hold of intellectually; comprehend. ... (*The American Heritage Dictionary*, 4th edition, 2000)

13) *Apprehend*: 1. To take into custody; arrest: *apprehended the murderer*. 2. To grasp mentally; understand: *a candidate who apprehends the significance of geopolitical issues*. ... (*The American Heritage Dictionary*, 4th edition, 2000)

Similarly, when we speak of *shelving* an old idea, we are using the metaphor of putting aside some useless physical object (like an out-of-date book) in reference to an idea, an abstract thing.14) Another instance of abstraction is *glad*, whose meaning changed from 'smooth' to 'a happy mental state'.

Many prefixes are spatial in their basic sense, but in most uses are metaphorically extended to express non-spatial meanings (Denning and Leben 1995: 99-100). The following table is a simplified version of Denning and Leben's (1995: 100) Table 7.2:

Table 6.2 Metaphoric Extensions of Meaning of Spatial Prefixes

Prefix	Spatial Sense	Use in Extended Sense
de-	down, away	*despair* (negative), *declare* (intensive)
pre-	in front of, forth	*precocious* (earlier)
sub-	below, under	*subsume* (as part), *subject* (open or exposed to)
per-	through	*pertinacious* (thorough, strong)
ex-	out, away	*expose* (open, visible), *except* (not included)
extra-	outside	*extraordinary* (not, beyond)
ob-	towards, down	*obloquy* (negative, destructive)

6.5. Objectivization and Subjectivization of Meaning

Meaning may be shift from subjective to objective (objectivization) and

---

14) *Shelve*: 1. To place or arrange on a shelf. 2. To put away as though on a shelf; put aside: "*As usual, Dixon shelved this question*" (Kingsley Amis). ... (*The American Heritage Dictionary*, 4th edition, 2000)

vice versa (subjectivization). The earlier meaning of *fear* was just 'danger', an objective concept, but its present meaning is subjective, describing 'a feeling of agitation and anxiety caused by the presence or imminence of danger'. *Pitiful* is the opposite case. Its former meaning was subjective describing the human mind 'filled with pity or compassion'. But now it is used to describe the objective situation, making people feel sympathy (e.g. *The refugees arriving at the camp had <u>pitiful</u> stories to tell*).

6.6. Broadening and Narrowing

Broadening is the phenomenon where the meaning of a word becomes more general. It is the widening, extending and generalizing of meaning, so broadening is sometimes termed extension or generalization, too. When the meaning of a word becomes broader, the range of the meanings of a word increases so that the word can mean everything it used to mean and more. For example, *mill* was formerly 'a place for making things by the process of grinding, that is making meal'.[15] Now it is simply 'a place for making things by any means, not by grinding only'. So we may speak of *a woolen <u>mill</u>, a steel <u>mill</u>* or even *a gin <u>mill</u>*.

  As we have already mentioned in Section 6.2, the main mechanism of broadening is, and possibly of the semantic change in general, is metaphor. Metaphor is the transfer of meaning based on an imagined similarity. The metonymic operation is another mechanism of the broadening of meaning, like the use of the word *foot* as a unit of measure. This again reveals that semantic changes may sometimes be of more than one type; broadening

---

15) Thus *meal* and *mill* are etymologically related to each other.

and metaphor, broadening and metonymy, and others.16) There are more examples of broadening in the following table:

Table 6.3 Broadening or Generalization

Words	Former Meaning	Present Meaning
dog	a particular breed of dog, a dog for hunting	dog in general (the species *canis familiaris*)
bird	a young bird	bird in general
clerk	a member of the clergy	clergyman, scholar, types of office worker, a shop/hotel worker (in AmE)
business	a state of being active (the state of being 'busy')	occupation, a piece of a concern /matter/affair, dealings, trade, a commercial enterprise
holiday	holy day (a day of religious significance)	any day on which we do not have to work
picture	painted representation	camera picture, movie (motion picture)
tail	hairy caudal appendage	caudal appendage
barn	a storehouse for barley (OE *bere* 'barley' + *ærn* 'house')	a storehouse for any kind of grain, a place for housing livestock
gentleman	a person of a high social class in England in the past	a man who is polite and behaves well towards other people
salary	a soldier's allotment of salt (Latin *salārium*)	a soldier's wages in general > wages in general

---

16) It should be bear in mind that "some types of semantic changes overlap with others, and some are defined only vaguely." This means that "some instances of semantic change will fit more than one type while others may fit none comfortably" (cf. Campbell (2001: 256)). Schendl (2001: 30) also says that "most existing classifications of semantic change are largely descriptive and based on various, partly overlapping criteria."

The inverse case to the broadening, i.e. the case where the meaning of a word becomes less general than formerly, is also found. This is the narrowing, restricting, specializing and limitation of meaning, so narrowing is sometimes termed specialization. This is a process in which the referential scope of a word reduced. For example, *a girl* formerly meant 'a young person of either sex, i.e. a child', and *meat* was 'food of any kind'.[17] But their present meanings are more specific. We have more examples of narrowing:

Table 6.4 Narrowing or Specialization

Words	Former Meaning	Present Meaning
meat	food in general	food of flesh
deer	animal in general (cf. Tier in German)	a particular four-legged wild animal
hound	dog in general (cf. Hund in German)	a dog for hunting
fowl	bird in general (OE fugol, cf. Vogel in German)	a bird of type that is edible or domestic
corn	grain (including e.g. oats and wheats, still in BrE)[18]	maize (in AmE)
liquor	fluid	alcoholic
starve	to die, (OE steorfan, cf. sterben in German)	to die of hunger or to suffer from hunger (cf. I'm starving. starving for love 'dying for love')
wife	woman	woman of low rank or of low employment[19] > a married woman

---

17) For example, the *meat* in such words as *mincemeat* or *sweetmeat* 'candy', where the original meaning remains, is not flesh.

6.7. Pejoration and Amelioration

In cases of broadening and narrowing, the sense or literal meaning(s) of a word changed. But a word may also undergo change in its connotations or associations. Such change was in many cases due to the changes of ethical or moral standards of the society. The meaning change can also be connected with the change of speaker evaluation. In other words, neutral, positive, or negative evaluations are subject to change. For example, the word *gay* had only the meaning of 'cheerful' and 'lively' until the middle of the last century.[20] But in the 1950s this word began to be used as a synonym for 'homosexual', and that is now its most usual sense. The degradation of meaning like this, caused by a negative evaluation, is called pejoration. The more examples of pejoration are given below:

---

18) *Corn*: 1a. Any of numerous cultivated forms of a widely grown, usually tall annual cereal grass (*Zea mays*) bearing grains or kernels on large ears. b. The grains or kernels of this plant, used as food for humans and livestock or for the extraction of an edible oil or starch. Also called *Indian corn, maize*. 2. An ear of this plant. 3. *Chiefly British* Any of various cereal plants or grains, especially the principal crop cultivated in a particular region, such as wheat in England or oats in Scotland. ... (*The American Heritage Dictionary*, 4th edition, 2000)
19) This meaning is observed in such words as *fishwife* 'an unpleasant offensive woman'.
20) There was a 19th-century nursery rhyme like this (Trask 1994: 41):

The child that is born on the Sabbath day
Is fair and wise, and good and gay.

Table 6.5 Pejoration or Degradation

Words	Former Meaning	Present Meaning
awful	being impressive or majestic (full of awe)[21]	extremely bad or unpleasant
villain, boor	farm worker	criminal, scoundrel
churl[22]	lowest rank of freeman	a rude, ill-bred person
knave	a child, a youth (cf. *Knabe* in German)	servant > a rogue
sinister	left, left-handed	making us feel that something bad or evil might happen
silly[23]	happy, blessed	foolish, stupid
lewd	ignorant	sexual in an obvious and rude way
lust	simple pleasure	sexual desire
vulgar	common	not in the style preferred by the upper classes of society
censure	opinion	strong criticism or disapproval

---

21) For this meaning, Present-day English uses the word *awesome*, particularly in American English.

22) *Churl* is from OE *ceorl* 'peasant, low ranking freeman. Germanic society was composed of mainly two ranks, *ceorl* and *eorl* (from which the title *earl* was derived).

23) "From its original meaning (<Old English *(ge)sælig* 'happy, blessed') attested till the late 15th century, *silly* passed through the following main stages: 'innocent' (late 13th c. - 18th c.) > 'deserving pity' (c. 1300 - 19th c.) > 'weak, feeble' (13th c. - 19th c.), 'simple, ignorant' (16th c. - c. 1800), 'feeble-minded' (16th c. - today), 'foolish, empty-minded' (late 16th c. - today). These dates illustrate that typically an old meaning is not replaced immediately by a new one, but that both coexist for some time, each in specific contexts." (Schendl 2001: 31) Words with multiple meanings, so-called polysemes, like *silly*, may lose a particular meaning in the course of time, so *silly* is the example of pejoration and at the same time the one of narrowing.

Meanwhile, the meaning can be elevated or get better. For example, the word *pretty* formerly had a negative sense of 'cunning, crafty'. Its present meaning is 'attractive and charming'. The shift in the sense of a word in the direction towards a more positive value is the amelioration or elevation of meaning.

Table 6.6 Amelioration or Elevation

Words	Former Meaning	Present Meaning
nice	silly, ignorant	pleasant, enjoyable or satisfactory
praise	put a value on, evaluate	value highly, express admiration or approval
knight	boy, servant (cf. *Knecht* in German)	military servant > a man given a rank of honor (by a British king or queen)
earl[24]	man (OE *eorl*)	a British man of high social rank
pretty	cunning, crafty, sly (OE *prættig*)	attractive, charming

6.8. Taboo and Euphemism

Another source of new meaning is the creation of euphemisms, which is the

---

[24] Many terms referring to women have undergone pejoration, while the corresponding terms for men have remained neutral or have improved, which mirrors the traditional lower status of women. (cf. Schendl (2001: 31); Campbell (2001: 262)). *Spinster* (from 'a woman who spins' to 'unmarried older woman'), *mistress* (from 'a woman who has the authority over servants or attendants' to 'a woman who is having a sexual relationship with a married man'), *madam* (from 'a polite form of address to woman' to 'the female head of a house of prostitution') are such examples.

replacement of words regarded as unpleasant. Euphemisms are polite but roundabout expressions for things which are considered too nasty to talk about directly. Such nasty words or expressions are called taboo terms. So euphemism is the replacement of a taboo term. For example, the verb *die* is too direct. Instead, such other expressions as *pass away, go west, kick the bucket, be no longer with us, expire, slip away, give up the ghost, go to sleep,* and others are used. However, euphemisms, in their turn, are often subject to pejoration, eventually becoming taboo. Thus we find a cyclic change in euphemisms. Euphemism is frequent when we come face to face with the less happy facts of our existence, or when we are talking about certain diseases, or humble occupations. Here are a few more euphemistic expressions:

Table 6.7 Euphemisms

The Intended Meaning	Euphemistic Expressions
urinate	*pass water, relieve oneself, have a wee, do number one, water the daisies, powder one's nose, see a man about a dog*
be a sexual partner of	*sleep with, be seeing, be going out with, be close friend of, be on intimate terms with*
kill	*liquidate, terminate* (with extreme prejudice), *remove, eliminate, dispose of, rub out, hit*[25]
death	*the Great Adventure, the flight to glory, the final sleep*
undertaker	*mortician*
toilet	> *lavatory* > WC > *rest room, comfort station, powder room, bath room, men's or women's room*
disease	*condition* (e.g. *heart condition, kidney condition, malignant condition*)
leprosy	*Hansen's disease*
elderly and decrepit people	*senior citizens*

poor	underprivileged, disadvantaged
insane	sick
doorkeeper	janitor, custodian, building worker, caretaker
garbage man	sanitary engineer

6.9. Semantic Bleaching

Another mechanism of meaning change is 'semantic bleaching', in which the original meaning of a word is bleached or grammaticalized into having a more functional or grammatical meaning. This process is connected with the process of grammaticalization. "Grammaticalization is the linguistic process whereby grammatical categories such as case or tense/aspect are organized and coded" (Traugott 1994: 1481). And "grammaticalization is generally seen as a process whereby a lexical item, with full referential meaning (i.e. an open-class element), develops grammatical meaning (i.e. it becomes a closed-class element); this is accompanied by a reduction in or loss of phonetic substance, loss of syntactic independence and of lexical (referential) meaning" (Fischer and Rosenbach 2000: 2). For example, English *will* was a full lexical verb, meaning 'want, wish, desire', but it was developed into the modern auxiliary verb, having grammatical meaning only.[26] Another example of grammaticalization is the development of the semi-auxiliary *going to*. The *going to* future originated by the extension of the spatial sense of the verb 'go' to a temporal sense. The original construction involved physical movement with an intention, such as *I am*

---

25) These expressions are all metaphoric expressions, too.
26) For the grammaticalization of English modals, refer to Section 5.3.2.1.

going [*outside*] *to harvest the crop*. The location later became unnecessary, and the expression was reinterpreted to represent a near future. The colloquial form *gonna* is a relaxed pronunciation of *going to*. For example, "This is gonna be awesome!". This shows one of the typical characteristics of grammaticalization, i.e. a phonetic reduction.

6.10. Why does Meaning Change?

The topic of why meanings change should be dealt with under the sub-topic of why language changes. As it is not easy to explain why language changes, so it is also difficult to account for why meanings change. Although we have seen in the above that there are several types of meaning change, the classifications of the types of meaning change do not say much about how and why these changes take place. Nevertheless, "some general statements about how and why meaning changes may be possible even if not all semantic changes are regular or predictable" (Campbell 2001: 267).

We have already mentioned several mechanisms affecting the meaning change, e.g. metaphoric and metonymic transfer, and the change of speaker's evaluation reflecting the changes in moral and ethnic values of the society. Then we ask why these mechanisms are employed. According to Schendl (2001: 32-34), several reasons may be conjectured. In the first place, "the need to adapt language to new communicative requirements" should be considered. To cover a new lexical demand, speakers often use existing words by extending its original meaning(s), without borrowing a word from a foreign source nor coining a new word. For example, a *mouse* originally refers to a kind of a small animal, but now it can refer to a computer device. This extension is again based on the metaphoric analogy.

Another, psychological factor in semantic change, argued by Schendl (2001: 32), is "a basic human tendency to emphasize and exaggerate."[27] The representative case is the continuous replacements of intensifying adverbs meaning 'very'. "Intensifiers constantly stand in need of replacement, because they are so frequently used that their intensifying force is worn down." (Pyles and Algeo 1993: 249-50). OE had an intensifying adverb *swīðe* (the adverbial form of *swīð* 'strong'), but it was replaced in ME by new intensifiers such as *full* and *right*. *Very* itself lost its independent meaning 'truly' and it has only intensifying function. Sometimes, the adverb *very* is replaced by a more 'stronger' one in PDE; *a very pleasant evening* > *an awfully pleasant evening, very nice* > *terribly nice*, and *very scared* > *horribly scared.* New intensifiers, like *too* (*You're too fat.*) and (*all*) *that* (*It wasn't* (*all*) *that good.*), are emerging constantly to meet a new need.

Another psychological factor in meaning change is the tendency to avoid direct reference to unpleasant or socially stigmatized concepts such as death, old age, illness and sexuality. The examples were given in Section 6.8.

From the language internal point of view, semantic change can be caused by the change in the meaning structure of groups of semantically related words (so-called semantic field). For example, in the case of the words like *bird/fowl* and *dog/hound*, a meaning change of one word affects the

---

27) Meaning exaggeration or overstatement is called **hyperbole** (from Greek *hyperboē* 'excess').

meaning of the other word. When the meaning of *hound* is narrowed from 'a dog in general' to 'a specific kind of dog', a new word signifying 'a dog in general' was needed, so the semantically related *dog* was adopted to deliver a new meaning, causing the broadening of the referential scope.

Some meaning changes are caused by the tendency for languages or speakers to avoid using two or more words with the exactly same meanings. Therefore, if two words have the same meanings, as in case of the borrowing of a word for which a synonymous native word exists, then one of them tends to disappear or to have different meanings or functions.

Although we have seen several factors leading to semantic change, we do not have any general principles of changes in word meaning. It is partly due to the fact that the systematic study of the linguistic meanings, i.e. semantics, is a relatively recent area.

6.11. Meaning Change and Dictionaries

We have seen that word meanings change in various ways. Although the examples given above are not comprehensive, they clearly show that the meanings of words are not constant. Therefore, we need to know the past meanings of a word as well as its present senses when we read the old documents (e.g. literary works). Otherwise, we could face with misinterpretation. Here, we can depend on such a big dictionary like *The Oxford English Dictionary* (*OED*) or its abbreviated version, *The Shorter Oxford English Dictionary* (*SOD*), where we can find all the meanings of an English word from its initial stage. *The OED*, published by the Oxford University Press (OUP), is the most comprehensive dictionary of the English language (20 big volumes). *The OED*'s policy was attempting the recording of a word's most-known usages and variants in all varieties of English past and present, world-wide. So it offers a wealth of information on individual word histories. The 1933 Preface says as follows:

> The aim of this Dictionary is to present in alphabetical series the words that have formed the English vocabulary from the time of the earliest records [ca. AD 740] down to the present day, with all the relevant facts concerning their form, **sense-history** (emphasis added), pronunciation, and etymology. It embraces not only the standard language of literature and conversation, whether current at the moment, or obsolete, or archaic, but also the main technical vocabulary, and a large measure of dialectal usage and slang.

So this dictionary will be the most important resource in discovering the past meanings of English words.

Cited Bibliography

I apologize for any possible infringement of copyright. I have tried to reveal the primary sources of the quotations, but it was limited and not always possible.

Aarts, B. 2001. *English Syntax and Argumentation,* 2nd edition. Basingstoke: Palgrave.

Barber, C. 1976. *Early Modern English.* London: Andre Deutsch.

_____. 1993. *The English Language: a Historical Introduction.* Cambridge: Cambridge University Press.

Baugh, A. and T. Cable. 1993. *A History of the English Language*, 4th edition. London: Routledge.

Bynon, T. 1994. Analogy. Asher, R. (ed). *Encyclopedia of Language and Linguistics*, 110-11. Oxford: Pergamon Press.

Campbell, L. 2001. *Historical Linguistics: An Introduction.* Cambridge, Massachusetts: MIT Press.

Carney, E. 1997. *English Spelling.* London and New York: Routledge.

Crystal, D. 2002. *The English Language: A Guided Tour of the Language*, 2nd edition. London: Penguin Books.

Culpeper, J. 1997. *History of English.* London and New York: Routledge.

Culpeper, J. and D. Archer. 2009. The History of English Spelling. Culpeper, J., F. Katambe, P. Kerswill, R. Woduk and T. McEnery. (eds). *English Language: Description, Variation and Context.* 244-58. New York: Palgrave Macmillan.

Denison, D. 1993. *English Historical Syntax.* London: Longman.

_____. 1998. Syntax. Romaine, S. (ed). *The Cambridge History of the English Language*, Vol 4, 1776-1997, 92-329. Cambridge: Cambridge University Press.

Denning, K and W. R. Leben. 1995. *English Vocabulary Elements.* Oxford: Oxford University Press.

Fischer, O. 1992. Syntax. Blake, N. (ed). *The Cambridge History of the English Language,* Vol 2, 1066-1476, 207-408. Cambridge: Cambridge University Press.

Fischer, O. and A. Rosenbach. 2000. Introduction. Fischer, O., A. Rosenbach and D. Stein (eds). *Pathways of Change: Grammaticalization in English,* 1-37. Amsterdam: John Benjamins.

Fischer, O and W. van der Wurff. 2006. Syntax. Hogg, R. and D. Denison (eds). *A History of the English Language,* 109-198. Cambridge: Cambridge University Press.

Fisiak, J. 1995. *An Outline History of English*, Vol 1. Poznan: Kantor Wydawniczy Saww.

Fromkin, V., R. Rodman and N. Hymes. 2003. *An Introduction to Language*, 7th edition. Boston: Thomson and Heinle.

Greenbaum, S. and R. Quirk. 1990. *A Student's Grammar of the English Language.* London: Longman.

Haegeman, L. 1991. *Introduction to Government and Binding Theory.* Oxford: Blackwell.

Hogg, R. (ed). 1992. *The Cambridge History of the English Language*, Vol 1. Cambridge: Cambridge University Press.

van Kemenade, A. 1987. *Syntactic Case and Morphological Case in the History* of English. Dordrecht: Foris.

Lee, P. H. 1993. *A Diachronic Study on Word Order in English: The Minimalist Approach*. PhD dissertation, Seoul National University.

_____. 1999a. *English Diachronic Syntax* (in Korean). Seoul: Hankookmunhwasa.

_____. 1999b. The Progressive Passives and the Extension of English Verbal Group: Functionalism vs. Formalism (in Korean). *History of English* 8, 63-92.

_____. 2007. *Syntactic Changes in English* (in Korean). Seoul: Hankookmunhwasa.

_____. 2008. On the Notion of Complement: To Advocate Fuzzy Grammar. *English Language and Linguistics* 25, 171-193.

Murphy, R. 2001. *Grammar in Use: Intermediate*, 2nd edition/2nd printing. Cambridge: Cambridge University Press.

Oxford English Dictionary = 1992 CD-ROM version. Oxford: Clarendon.

Pintzuk, S. 1991. *Phrase Structures in Competition: Variation and Change in Old English Word Order*. PhD dissertation, University of Pennsylvania.

Quirk, R., S. Greenbaum, G. Leech, and S. Svartvik. 1985. *A Comprehensive Grammar of the English language*. London: Longman.

Pyles, T. and J. Algeo. 1993. *The Origins and Development of the English Language*, 4th edition. New York: Harcourt Brace Jovanovich.

Rastall, P. 2002. English in a Historical Perspective - a Neglected Inheritance. *English Today* 70, Vol 18, No. 2, 28-32.

Rissanen, M. 1999. Syntax. Lass, R. (ed). *The Cambridge History of the English Language*, Vol 3, 1476-1776, 187-331. Cambridge: Cambridge University Press.

Robinson, F. C. 1994. Old English. Asher, R. (ed). *Encyclopedia of Language and Linguistics*, 2868-71. Oxford: Pergamon Press.

Schendl, H. 2001. *Historical Linguistics*. Oxford: Oxford University Press.

Smith, J. J. 1994. Middle English. Asher, R. (ed). *Encyclopedia of Language and Linguistics*, 2487-91. Oxford: Pergamon Press.

Svartvik, J. and G. Leech. 2006. *English: One tongue, Many Voices*. New York: Palgrave MacMillan.

Trask, R. L. 1994. *Language Change*. London and New York: Routledge.

_____. 2010. *Why Do Languages Change*? (Revised by Robert McColl Millar). Cambridge: Cambridge University Press.

Traugott, E. C. 1972. *The History of English Syntax: A Transformational Approach to the History of English Sentence Structure*. New York: Holt, Rinehart and Winston.

_____. 1994. Grammaticalization and Lexicalization. Asher, R. (ed). *Encyclopedia of Language and Linguistics*, 1481-86. Oxford: Pergamon Press.

Wikipedia, the Free Encyclopedia. http://en.wikipedia.org/wiki.

Index

a

a-stem declension 103, 104
abstraction of meaning 170
accommodation 15
accusative case 83, 127, 158
acronym 44
affixation 40
affixes 32, 40, 41
affricate 36, 70
amelioration 175, 177
analogy 17, 18, 181
analytical language 83
Anglo-Norman 35
anomalous verbs 114
ash 57
aspect 84, 112, 138
associations 167, 175
auxiliaries 132, 136

b

back formation 45
back vowel 70, 71
be-perfect 143
Bernard Shaw 79
blends 43
bound morphemes 41
British Celts 23
broadening 172

c

Central French 35
Christianity 28, 49
clipping 44
code-switching 11
compounds 41
conjugation 81, 84, 112
connotations 175
connotative meaning 166

d

dative case 83, 158
declensions 81, 83, 101, 106
demonstratives 99
denotative meaning 166
derivation 40
determiner 125, 128
diagraph 64
dictionaries 55, 165, 182

digraph	66
do-support	147
double *be*	149
doublets	35
dual number	88
dummy subject	154

e

economy	18
elevation	177
eponyms	45
euphemism	177
Experiencer	157

f

finite verb-forms	134
French	33
fricatives	71
front vowel	70, 71
functional shift	43

g

generalization	172
genitive	83, 158
Geographical separation	14
Germanic languages	111
grammatical conversion	43
grammatical function	15, 81, 153
grammatical gender	84
grammatical word	126

grammaticalization	16, 138, 179
Great Vowel Shift	56, 74
Greek	30, 32
Gregory	28

h

head	125
his	94
his-genitive	105

i

Impersonal Constructions	157
impersonal passive	162
Indirect Passive	160
Indo-European languages	111
Inflection	81
inflectional language	15
inflectional passive	144
inflections	113, 124
instrumental	83
inversion	122
Irish Gaelic	23
its	93

j

Jamestown	13
John Hart	77
Jutes	23

Index 189

k

King James Bible ············ 68, 93, 94

l

language change ············ 9, 10
language contact ············ 11, 21, 121
Latin ············ 27, 49
Latin alphabet ············ 50, 53, 59
lexical change ············ 21
lexical verb ············ 134, 137, 148
lexical word ············ 125
linguistic accommodation ············ 14
loanwords ············ 13, 22

m

meaning ············ 179
metaphor ············ 167, 172
metonymy ············ 168, 173
Middle English ············ 12
modal auxiliaries ············ 136
Modern English ············ 12
modifiers ············ 125
mood ············ 84, 112
morphological change ············ 81
multiple negation ············ 151
mutation ············ 103

n

narrowing ············ 174

n (continued)

natural gender ············ 84
negation ············ 151
negative adverb ············ 152
neologisms ············ 44
Noah Webster ············ 79
nominative case ············ 127
nonce formation ············ 40
nonfinite verb-forms ············ 134
Norman Conquest ············ 23, 33, 54
Norman French ············ 35
Normans ············ 12

o

objective case ············ 83, 86, 127
objectivization ············ 171
of it ············ 94
Old French ············ 36
Old Norse ············ 23, 25, 85
Oxford English Dictionary ············ 182

p

pejoration ············ 175
Perfective ············ 142
Perfective-Progressive-Passive ············ 148
Perfective-Passive ············ 133, 148
Perfective-Progressive ············ 133, 148
Perfective-Progressive-Passive ············ 133
periphrastic passive ············ 144
phonemes ············ 71
possessive case ············ 83, 86

pre-modals ················· 137
predicate ················· 118
prefixes ················· 41, 171
prepositional passive ········· 160
printing ················· 55
pro-drop ················· 155
Progressive ················· 139
Progressive-Passive ········· 133, 148
Proto-Germanic ·············· 111

r

reanalysis ················· 17
Renaissance ·········· 23, 30, 32
Richard Mulcaster ············ 78
Roman Empire ········ 28, 29, 32, 49
root creation ················ 40
Runes ··················· 50

s

Samuel Johnson ··············· 56
Scandinavian invasions ········· 12, 24
schwa ··················· 76, 104
Scottish Gaelic ··············· 23
semantic bleaching ············ 179
semantic change ·············· 165
senses ···················· 167
Shorter Oxford English Dictionary ··· 182
Source ···················· 157
SOV ····················· 123
specialization ················ 174

spelling change ··············· 56
spelling reforms ··············· 77
St. Augustine ················· 28
strong verb ·············· 111, 112
subjective case ········ 83, 86, 127
subjectivization ··············· 172
suffixes ····················· 41
suppletion ··················· 115
synecdoche ·················· 169
synesthesia ·················· 169
synonyms ················· 37, 42
syntactic change ············· 117

t

taboo ···················· 177
tense ················ 84, 112, 135
that ················ 97, 100, 130
that-those ··················· 99
the ······················· 99
thereof ···················· 94
this-these ··················· 99
thorn ··················· 59, 67
thou ······················ 91
transfer of meaning ··········· 167

v

Verb-Second ················ 120
verbal group ················ 132
Vikings ················ 12, 24, 113

Index 191

W

weak verb 111, 112
Welsh 23
weorþan construction 145
what 95
who 95

Y

yogh 64, 67
Yon(d(er)) 130